CEF Level B2

the
grammar
files

English Usage

Upper - Intermediate

GlobalELT
ENGLISH LANGUAGE TEACHING BOOKS

Grammar Files

CEF Level B2

Published by GLOBAL ELT LTD
www.globalelt.co.uk
email: orders@globalelt.co.uk
Copyright © **GLOBAL ELT LTD**

The right of Lawrence Mamas & Andrew Betsis to be identified as the authors
of this work has been asserted in accordance with the Copyright, Designs and Patent Act 1988. /2012

British Library Cataloguing-in-Publication Data

Components:
- Grammar Files - Level B2 - Teacher's Book - ISBN: 978-1-904663-54-6
- Grammar Files - Level B2 - Student's Book - ISBN: 978-1-904663-53-9

CONTENTS

Unit 1

Who? / What? / Which?

Ask questions with:

Who
        about a person

Which (+of)
        about a person or thing

What
        about things, actions, ideas, opinions, jobs, etc

Use **who** and **what** when there is a limitless number of people or things to choose from.
- *Who's your sister?*
- *What's your favourite radio station?*

Use **which** when there is a limited choice.
- *Which (of the girls in the picture) is your sister?*

Note: **Which** and **what**, but NOT **who**, may be used before nouns.
- *Which car is yours?*
- *What colour is it?*
- *Who came? but not Who girl came?*

Fill in the gaps with <u>who, which, what</u>.

1 _____ would you like to speak to?

2 _____ department do you want, sir?

3 _____ do you mean?

4 _____ student answered the question?

5 _____ DVD did you buy?

6 _____ has been invited to the party?

7 _____ does he do?

8 'I got a letter from Brian today.'
'Brian _____?'

Uncountable nouns

i **a.** They may refer to liquids *(oil)*, things we eat *(sugar)*, abstract ideas *(news, information)*, natural materials *(gold, cotton)*.
  b. Some common uncountable nouns do not come under the categories above: *furniture, money, hair, luggage*

ii. They have only one form and cannot normally be used with the indefinite article **a / an** or with numbers.

iii. They may come after words like **the, some, any, no, much, this/that, little, my/your.**
- *There's not much bread left.*
- *I have little information to give to you, I'm afraid.*

iv. When they become the subject of the verb, the verb is in the singular.
- *The furniture we bought was rather expensive.*

v. Some nouns may be either countable or uncountable depending on the meaning:
- *I've bought a paper (=newspaper).* **but**
  There is some paper on my desk(=to write on).

vi. Another way to show quantity with uncountable nouns is to use words that describe them as units such as *piece, bit, bar, glass, tin, packet, loaf, sheet* together with **of**.
- *Ten sheets of paper.*
- *A useful piece of advice.*

Use the prompts to make sentences, changing the verb form where necessary.

1 he / give / me / very / useful / advice.
_____

2 news / be / really / worrying.
_____

3 you / have / luggage?
_____

4 there / be / fruit / but / there / be / no / vegetables.
_____

5 money / be / in / the / drawer.
_____

6 not / forget / to buy / two / soap.
_____

7 there / be / egg / on / my dress.
_____

Present Continuous vs. Present Simple

Use the **Present Continuous (*I am doing*)** for:

a. an activity that is in progress now,
- *You can't speak to John. He's having a bath.*

b. temporary states,
- *I'm living with my brother until I find a place of my own.*

c. habits which are considered annoying, together with **always, forever, constantly**.
- *You're always coming home late.*

Use the **Present Simple (*I do*)** for:

a. a habitual or repeated action,
- *She goes to school every day.*

b. facts or permanent states.
- *Water boils at 100° C.*
- *She lives in Paris.*

Decide whether the underlined verbs are right or wrong. Correct the mistakes.

1 Although he is a chemist, <u>he works</u> as a waiter at the moment.

_____

2 I'm afraid <u>the hotels are costing</u> too much and we can't afford it.

_____

3 'Where is John?' 'I think <u>he is talking</u> to Susan on the phone.'

_____

4 <u>Are you ever visiting</u> your brother in Australia?

_____

5 <u>Do you often have</u> coffee in the morning?

_____

do, does and did

do, does and **did** are used:

i. as **AUXILIARY VERBS**:

a. to form questions and negative statements in the Simple Present and Simple Past,
- *Doesn't/Does she like ice-cream?*
- *Her parents didn't allow her to go to the dance.*

b. to form the negative imperative,
- *Don't switch the TV off yet.*

c. to add emphasis,
- *He does know her quite well.*

d. to avoid repeating a main verb.
- *I thought they would come, but they didn't.*

ii. as **MAIN VERBS** meaning:

a. to carry out an action which is not specified or not yet known,
- *What shall I do?*
- *They aren't doing anything at the moment.*

b. to perform a task or activity. In this case **do** is followed by **the + noun / the + ing,**
- *You do the windows. I'll do the washing up.*

c. to work at,
- *He has done all kinds of jobs in his life.*

d. to study for.
- *He did his MA at London University.*

Rearrange the words to make full sentences. Indicate whether <u>do</u> is used as an auxiliary (Aux) or main verb (MV).

1 why / your / exam results / do / about / lie / to / always / me / you?

_____

2 don't / dusting / mind / I / doing / you / if / do / the / hoovering / the.

_____

3 tell / you / you / but / did / do / I / not / remember.

_____

4 school / at / did / history / he.

_____

5 panic/ not / do.
sure / can / you / do / I / manage / am / to / it.

_____

6 afternoon / what / this / doing / you / are?

_____

7 do / boyfriend / I / not / my / enjoys / but / abroad / travelling.

_____

Exercise 1

For questions 1 -9, read the text below and look carefully at each line. Some of the lines are correct, and some have a word which should not be there. If a line is correct, put a tick (✓) by the number. If a line has a word that should not be there, write the word next to the number.

Film Review - JUNIOR

1 Arnold Schwarzenegger makes fun of his tough-guy image by is playing
2 the world's first pregnant man. Yes, folks - Arnold pregnant. Arnold wear in
3 a pink dress. Arnold with women's problems. Oh boy! Now what, depending
4 on your point of view, this is either very upsetting or really much funny.
5 Devoted fans of Arnold's action days they are likely to be disappointed with
6 'Junior'. But if you enjoyed his first two comedies, this one shouldn't will
7 come as too much of a surprise. Directed by Ivan Reitman, this is a light,
8 silly comedy, though be worth watching and reasonably entertaining. Maybe
9 even funny, if after 'Mrs Doubtfire' you can to still laugh at a man in
women's clothing.

Exercise 2

For questions 10 - 17, use the word given in capitals at the end of each line to form a word that fits in the space in the same line.

GADGET MANIA

Collecting gadgets doesn't seem to be a(n) (10) .... thing. There — USUAL
probably isn't a (11) .... in the land that hasn't got a drawer filled — HOUSE
with an (12) .... of small devices ranging from egg separators to new and — ASSORT
(13) .... mousetraps. Gadgets promise short cuts, ease, efficiency — EFFECT
and (14) .... Although they are probably the inevitable by-products — FREE
of the (15) .... revolution, they also represent little in terms of — INDUSTRY
(16) .... progress. When people stop using old-fashioned utensils, — TECHNOLOGY
gadget (17) .... begins. — ADDICT

Exercise 3

For questions 18 - 27, read the text below and think of the word which fits each space. Use only one word in each space.

WITH A LITTLE BIT OF HELP

The ozone layer (18) .... becoming thinner all over the world. 70% of Antarctica's ozone blanket has already disappeared. (19) .... means that people, plants and animals are in more danger of suffering (20) .... skin cancers and diseases. Who is (21) .... blame? Who is slowly destroying our only protection against the sun's dangerous ultraviolet rays? We are.

The destruction of the ozone layer is mostly caused (22) .... man-made chemicals like CFCs, which are used as coolants in refrigerators and air-conditioning systems or in sprays. Every time you (23) .... on an air-conditioning system manufactured with CFCs, you are (24) .... something to destroy the ozone layer. Every time you spray styling foam on your hair, you are making the ozone layer a (25) .... bit thinner.

But there is a bright side to this. Many chemical companies are producing less CFCs. (26) .... a few years' time, the amount of CFCs in the atmosphere will have started to drop, and if countries cooperate fully by not manufacturing more CFCs, the ozone layer will have fully recovered by the year 2050.

In some European countries, 'green' refrigerators are (27) .... manufactured without CFCs, which have already replaced 50% of the market.

Exercise 4

For questions 28 - 32, complete the second sentence so that it has a similar meaning to the first sentence, using the word given.
Do not change the word given.

28 Mr Smith is free at the moment. Would you like to speak to him? Mr Smith .... Would you like to speak to him?	**doing**
29 Just add a pinch of salt to the soup. Just .... to the soup.	**little**
30 My father cooks dinner every Friday evening. My father .... every Friday evening.	**does**
31 I'm having difficulty choosing between the red dress and the black dress. I don't know .... : the red one or the black one.	**which**
32 After having her hair dyed a few times, she noticed that she had less hair than before. After having her hair dyed a few times, she noticed that she didn't .... before.	**much**

Phrasal verbs

put...away
  return to its rightful place
put...off
  postpone
put...on
  i. get dressed; wear
  ii. switch on
put...out
  extinguish
put...through
  make a connection on the phone
put...up
  i. raise (the price)
  ii. provide accommodation
put up with
  tolerate

Fill in the gaps with the appropriate phrasal verb.

1 No matter how hard they tried, they couldn't _____ the fire.

2 Will you _____ me _____ for the night?

3 I'm afraid we'll have to _____ this meeting until tomorrow.

4 _____ your toys _____ and go to bed right now!

5 I'm not prepared to _____ his bad temper.

6 _____ your coat. It's time for us to go.

7 Hold on. I'll _____ you _____ to the manager.

8 I'll _____ the music and you can pour the wine.

9 They've _____ the price of petrol again.

during vs. while

during + noun indicates:
i. that sth happens over a period of time or several times from the beginning to the end of that period,
  ■ *He phoned several times during your absence.*

ii. that sth happens at some point in a certain period of time.
  ■ *I fell asleep during the film.*

while + subject + verb means during the time that.
  ■ *I saw him while I was crossing the street.*

Use during, or while to fill in the blanks.

1 I used to see him quite often _____ he was in Athens.

2 Mary often goes skiing _____ the winter.

3 It rained heavily _____ the night.

4 I met an old friend of mine _____ I was waiting for the bus.

5 _____ he was on holiday, he met a famous writer.

Nouns ending in -ics

All nouns that refer to fields of study are uncountable, even if they end in **-ics.** They are, therefore, followed by a verb in the singular.
  ■ *Economics is the study of the production and distribution of money and goods.*
  ■ *History was my favourite subject at school.*

LEARNING TIPS

Learn the correct noun form for a field of study and the job title of the person who works in that field.

Match 1-4 with A-D to make complete sentences. Put the verb in the correct tense.

  1 French   **2** Physics   **3** Linguistics   **4** Maths

A (include) _____ the study of magnetic fields.

B (involve) _____ the study of numbers, quantities, shapes, etc.

C (study) _____ the way in which language works.

D (be) _____ one of his favourite subjects at high school.

Past Continuous vs. Simple Past

Use the **Past Continuous (I was doing)** to describe:
i. an activity which was in progress at a certain point of time in the past,
   - *When I saw them, they were playing tennis.*
ii. (usually with **while**) two parallel activities happening at the same time in the past.
   - *He was playing the piano while she was trying to study.*

Use the **Simple Past (I did)** to describe:
i. an action that was completed in the past at a definite time,
   - *He finished his studies a couple of years ago.*
ii. complete actions in the past that follow one another,
   He first examined the patient and then gave him some medicine to relieve the pain.
iii. a habitual action in the past.
   - *I studied every day when I was at school.*

The **Past Continuous** and **Simple** can be used in the same sentence to describe a longer action which was interrupted by a briefer one.
   - *I was having a bath when I heard the fire alarm.*

Decide whether the underlined verbs are RIGHT or WRONG. Correct the mistakes.

1. Although I was starting early, I didn't manage to finish it.

_____

2. Where did you lose your passport?

_____

3. Ken rode his bike to work when he was living in Chesham.

_____

4. When I saw her, she was telling me about her accident.

_____

5. I was feeding the baby while Ann prepared dinner.

_____

6. What did you do at the time of the murder?

_____

Stative and Dynamic verbs

Stative verbs:
i. describe feelings or states,
   - *Do you understand?*

ii. are not usually used in continuous tenses.

Dynamic verbs:
i. describe actions,
   - *He frequently talks to her on the phone.*
ii. can be used in continuous tenses.
   - *He is talking on the phone at the moment.*

Note: Certain verbs can be both stative and dynamic depending on:

i. the meaning,
   - *I see what you mean. (stative)*
   - *I'm seeing him on Monday. (dynamic)*

ii. whether or not the subject has any control over the action.
   - *We will face a lot of changes over the next few months. (stative)*
   - *The teacher was facing the class. (dynamic)*

Use the prompts to construct sentences.

1. The food / smell / good. I / think / I / try / some / now.

_____

2. John / be / absent-minded / because / he / think / about / his girlfriend.

_____

3. Of course / I / know / Johnny Depp. He / be / brilliant / actor.

_____

4. It / now / seem / certain / accident / be / his fault.

_____

5. She / appear / on / talk / show / TV / tonight.

_____

Unit 2

Exercise 1

For questions 1 - 9, read the text below and look carefully at each line. Some of the lines are correct, and some have a word which should not be there. If a line is correct, put a tick (✓) by the number. Otherwise, write the word next to the number.

ROBINSON CRUSOE, SCOTTISH PIRATE

1 Daniel Defoe's 'Robinson Crusoe' might never would have been written if it hadn't
2 been for a quarrel that Alexander Selkirk had on a Scottish pirate ship in
3 one night in 1704. During a voyage to the South Seas, Selkirk had an
4 argument with the captain and demanded to be put ashore. The captain did
5 left him to ashore - on an uninhabited island off the coast of Chile.
6 Nobody knows for what the row was about. But it meant that Selkirk had to
7 live on the island for nearly four and a half years ago, until he was rescued
8 in 1709 and returned to England. Being a journalist, Defoe heard about
9 Selkirk, and used the pirate's story as much the basis of his own story which was
   about a religious man who was abandoned on a desert island for 24 years.

Exercise 2

For questions 10-17, read the text below. Use the word given in capitals to form a word that fits in the space in the same line.

I have never been a very (10) .... person. However, a close friend finally persuaded me to take up jogging. An easy and (11) .... form of exercise, or so he said. Equipped with the latest jogging gear, complete with headband and walkman, I set off for the park. Nobody had told me any-thing about warming up first or how to avoid leg (12) .... Twenty minutes into my first, and last, attempt at jogging, I did what every first-timer's nightmares are made of. I tripped and found myself lying (13) .... in front of several other 'seasoned' joggers. Of course, I had to get out of this embarrassing situation as quickly and discreetly as possible. So, (14) .... any offers of help and despite a (15) .... ankle, I continued running... straight home. The next morning every muscle in my body was sore, even muscles I didn't know I even had, and I could hardly walk. My doctor promised me that the (16) .... in my muscles would go away in a couple of days but I would have to get (17) .... for my ankle and that would probably include some time off work. Then and there I decided that jogging was not for me.

ATHLETE

HARM

INJURE

BREATH

REGARD

PAIN

STIFF

TREAT

Exercise 3

For questions 18 - 24, read the text below and think of the word which fits each space. Use only one word in each space.

A GHOSTLY WARNING

While staying at a friend's house in Ireland, Lord Dufferin was suddenly awoken (18) .... the night. Going to the window, he saw a man carrying what looked (19) .... a coffin. When he shouted from the window, the man looked up and Lord Dufferin saw a wrinkled, ugly face that totally disgusted him. He turned away but when he looked back, the man had disappeared. A few years (20) .... , Lord Dufferin was in Paris for a party at the Grand Hotel. Just as he was about to enter the lift, Dufferin took a step back and refused to go inside. The lift operator was none other (21) .... the ugly man he had seen in Ireland years before. (22) .... the lift was on its way up, Lord Dufferin went to the reception desk to find out who the strange man was. Then something tragic happened. Seconds before the lift (23) .... the fifth floor, the cable snapped killing all (24) .... occupants. The hotel management couldn't find any record of the lift operator's name or background.

Exercise 4

For questions 25 - 29, complete the second sentence so that it has a similar meaning to the first one, using the word given. Do not change the word given.

25 I have arranged to meet Mrs Williams tomorrow. I .... Mrs Williams tomorrow.	seeing
26 While he was staying in Egypt, he visited the pyramids. He visited the pyramids .... in Egypt.	during
27 I am sure that ghosts don't exist. I .... ghosts.	believe
28 I was very bad at economics when I was at school. Economics .... when I was at school.	worst
29 It started to rain in the middle of their picnic. It started to rain .... a picnic.	having

Phrasal verbs

go after
    pursue, follow
go by
    pass
go down with
    become ill
go in for
    start having an interest in
go on
    continue
go out
    stop burning
go over
    examine carefully and systematically
go through
    suffer, endure
go with
    match, suit

Fill in the gaps with the appropriate phrasal verb in the correct tense.

1. After a short introduction, he _____ to talk about various local issues.

2. She has _____ a lot lately and I think she deserves a holiday.

3. As time _____ , we became more and more anxious.

4. The moment the earthquake struck, all the lights _____ .

5. I don't think that this Persian rug _____ the curtains.

6. I've _____ these figures twice and I still can't find the error.

7. The baby _____ a cold last week but she's feeling better now.

8. He _____ her when she rushed out of the cafe.

9. My brother is thinking of _____ basketball this season.

still, yet, already

<u>Still</u> in affirmative, interrogative and negative sentences means that the action continues. It usually comes BEFORE the verb, but after forms of the verb to be.
- *I'm still working on the same project.*
- *Are you still interested in doing an MA?*
- *She still hasn't received the report I sent her.*

<u>Yet</u> in negative and interrogative sentences means: *'up to the time of speaking'*. It usually comes AT THE END of the sentence.
- *Have you finished yet?*
- *It's not ready yet.*

Note: **Still** may be used instead of **yet** in negative sentences to place special emphasis on the negative.
- *It isn't still raining. It has already stopped.*
- *I still haven't finished typing those letters.*

<u>Already</u> in affirmative sentences means: *'by this/that time'*. It usually comes before the main verb but it can also come at the end of the sentence. It may be used at the end of questions to express surprise.
- *I've already read this book, so you can borrow it.*
- *Are you leaving already?*

Correct the mistakes in the sentences below.

1. I yet haven't found the answer to that question.

_____

2. He hasn't been to the bank still.

_____

3. I don't want to see that film. I have seen it yet.

_____

4. I've been to Venice several times but I already get lost.

_____

5. Despite working hard, Bob is yet making mistakes.

_____

Objects with two identical parts

i. These nouns are always in the plural
   ■ *trousers, glasses, pliers, binoculars, tweezers, etc*

ii. The verb that follows these nouns is in the plural form too
   ■ *Your jeans are dirty. You'd better wash them.*

iii. To refer to one or several items, use the expression *pair (of)*
   ■ *a pair of jeans, four pairs of jeans*
   ■ *a pair of scissors*

Match the phrases 1-4 with the phrases A-D to make complete sentences.

1 My white shoes are dirty

2 My daughter's new shorts

3 The scissors he used to kill the victim

4 I don't think his new sunglasses

A were found in a drawer.

B suit him.

C so I'll have to wash them.

D are too small so I've got to take them back.

Present Perfect Simple vs. Present Perfect Continuous

The **Present Perfect Simple** (*I have done*) is used to describe an action:

i. that happened in the past at a time which is not specified and the result comes up to the present,
   ■ *I've washed the dishes. (The dishes are clean now.)*
ii. that happened once or more than once within an unfinished period of time
   (e.g. this week, this afternoon),
   ■ *I've seen him twice this morning. (It is still morning.)*
   Compare:
   ■ *I saw him twice this morning.*
   (Now it's afternoon or evening.)
iii. that was recently completed. In this case use **just** or **recently** before the past participle.
   ■ *Raymond has just finished his homework.*

The **Present Perfect Continuous** (*I have been doing*) is used to describe an action:

i. which is in progress at the moment of speaking but also extends backwards into the past for a specified period of time
   ■ *She's been working for the same company for six years / since 1997.*
ii. which finished only a short time ago (the results are clearly seen or felt at the moment of speaking)
   ■ *Why are you breathless? Have you been running?*

Note: *Yet* and *already* are often used with the Present Perfect.
   ■ *Haven't you finished yet?*
   ■ *I've already read that book, so you can borrow it.*

Decide whether the underlined verbs are right or wrong. Correct the mistakes.

1 I <u>have waited</u> for you since ten o'clock.

_____

2 <u>Have</u> you <u>already finished</u> your homework?

_____

3 Watch out! <u>I have just been painting</u> the door.

_____

4 I look tired because <u>I have been working</u> really hard today.

_____

5 John <u>has been seeing</u> Ann twice this week.

_____

6 <u>He has known</u> her for a year.

_____

7 <u>Have</u> you <u>seen</u> the film *The Lord of the Rings* yet?

_____

13

Unit 3

Exercise 1

For questions 1 - 11, read the text below and look carefully at each line. Some of the lines are correct, and some have a word which should not be there. If a line is correct, put a tick (✓) by the number. If a line has a word that should not be there, write the word next to the number.

THE BARBIE DOLL IMAGE

1	Psychologists have yet long believed that repeated exposure to images of	
2	thin women on magazine covers, on TV shows and in films is been linked to	
3	the rising incidence of eating disorders. Researchers did surveyed 238	
4	women and discovered that those with the most exposure to 'ideal' body	
5	images in the media were most likely to display eating-disorder symptoms.	
6	These women tended to hide their desire to be model-thin. Making the	
7	matters worse, is the fact that this too-slender goal is not only unhealthy,	
8	but almost hardly impossible to achieve since only one in 10,000 females	
9	biologically meets model-thin standards. However, the media is not fully	
10	entirely to blame. When family members and peers suggest that one has so	
11	put on weight and needs to go on a diet, they reinforce the thin ideal, too.	

Exercise 2

For questions 12 - 17, read the text below. Use the word given in capitals at the end of each line to form a word that fits in the space in the same line.

WHAT ARE WE CHEWING?

How (12) .... was chewing gum when it was first discovered?   EAT

The (13) .... base of chewing gum was found in the Sapodilla tree in South   ORIGIN

America. Americans travelled to South America on the (14) .... that this base   ASSUME

could be used in the (15) .... of synthetic rubber. However, after many   PRODUCT

(16) .... , attempts to improve its elasticity were abandoned. Finally, a Mr Adams   FAIL

discovered a (17) .... way to use it and thought of selling it as chewing gum.   PROFIT

Exercise 3

For questions 18 - 26, read the text below and think of the word which fits each space. Use only one word in each space.

WAKING UP TO FOOD

Do you skip breakfast? Lots of people do because (18) .... years we've been (19) .... mixed signals about eating breakfast. On the one hand, we've been told that it's critical for good health; on the (20) .... , we've been informed that it's more of an option than a necessity. However, there is growing evidence that your body needs a nutritious wake-up call. Research has found that people who don't (21) .... something at the start of the day have higher levels of cholesterol than those who do, and they tend to eat (22) .... throughout the day to make up for what they missed in the morning. What's (23) .... , if you skip breakfast you (24) .... the risk of missing out on important nutrients such as fibre in cereals and whole-grain breads, vitamins from juice or fruit and calcium in milk. So, try (25) .... some orange juice in the morning instead of coffee and have a bowl of cereal instead of running out the door saying 'No time to eat. I've got to run.' You may (26) .... that you'll get more out of breakfast cereal than just the special prize in the box.

Exercise 4

For questions 27 - 31, complete the second sentence so that it has a similar meaning to the first sentence, using the word given. Do not change the word given.

27 The police haven't yet located the suspect involved in the bank robbery.   **still**
    The police .... the suspect involved in the bank robbery.

28 Researchers have recently completed their latest survey into European eating habits.   **just**
    Researchers .... their latest survey into European eating habits.

29 Maria has just given birth to triplets.   **had**
    Maria .... triplets.

30 John's been working on his school project since last week.   **for**
    John's .... week.

31 We enjoyed your party very much.   **time**
    We .... party.

Unit 4

Phrasal verbs

look after
    take care of
look (a)round
    view; inspect
look for
    search for, seek
look in
    visit briefly
look into
    investigate
look out (for)
    pay attention in order to notice
    sth when it occurs
look through
    examine; inspect
look...up
    try to find information
    (in a dictionary, etc)
look up to
    respect

Fill in the gaps with the appropriate phrasal verb in the correct tense.

1 Store detectives are constantly _____ shoplifters.

2 Where on earth is he? I _____ him all morning.

3 Will you _____ my pet snake while I'm away?

4 He was fine when I last _____ on him a few days ago.

5 We'll give you an answer as soon as we _____ the matter.

6 _____ the Tate Gallery took us almost six hours.

7 He's a prominent scientist and his colleagues _____ _____ him.

8 I haven't had the time to _____ the books you gave me.

9 Sharon spent the morning _____ words in the dictionary.

for, since

For + [a period of time] indicates the length of time.

  ■ *I've known him for five years.*

Since + [a point in past time] indicates the point in the past when sth started.

  ■ *I've known him since 1990.*

When **since** is followed by a verb, the verb should be in the simple past.

  ■ *I've known him since I left school.*

Fill in the gaps with <u>for</u> or <u>since</u>.

1 He's been working as a clerk _____ nine months.

2 She hasn't been anywhere else _____ she visited Paris.

3 I've been cleaning the house _____ nine o'clock this morning.

4 I've owned this house _____ ten years.

/the/ vs. /zero article/

Use **the**:

i. with something already mentioned,
   ■ *He wrote her a letter. However, the letter was never posted.*

ii. with nouns that refer to unique things
   ■ *the sun, the moon*

iii. with adjectives referring to groups of people sharing the same characteristics or qualities
   ■ *Special facilities are provided for the blind.*

iv. with names of countries or groups of islands which are plural
   ■ *the Netherlands, the Bahamas*

v. with names of rivers, oceans and seas
   ■ *the Nile, the Pacific, the Mediterranean.*

Use **zero article**, with the names of:

i. people ■ *John arrived yesterday.*

ii. towns ■ *It usually takes two hours to get to London.*

iii. roads ■ *Where's Oxford Street?*

iv. countries ■ *Paris is the capital of France.*

v. lakes ■ *Great Bear is the largest lake in Canada.*

vi. individual islands ■ *Sicily is part of Italy.*

vii. institutions ■ *My bank account is with HSBC Bank.*

viii. meals ■ *I've invited some friends to dinner.*

ix. games ■ *He used to play basketball a lot.*

Fill in the gaps with the or zero article.

1. They had _____ dinner at a restaurant near _____ theatre.

2. He's studying Chemistry at _____ Manchester University.

3. Priscilla lives in _____ Paris but she often visits _____ USA.

4. _____ rich should help _____ poor.

5. Why don't we travel to _____ Mediterranean and visit Crete?

6. I thought that _____ Dr Collins would be going with us.

7. Would you like to join us for a game of _____ football on Saturday?

8. According to _____ police, no one was to blame for the accident.

9. Have you heard? There will be a total eclipse of _____ moon this coming Monday.

10. My house is on _____ corner of Baily Rd and _____ York Avenue.

11. The largest lake in the world is _____ Lake Victoria in East Africa.

Present Perfect Simple vs. Simple Past

Note the difference between the **Present Perfect (I have done)** and the **Simple Past (I did)**:

Use the **Present Perfect**:	Use the **Simple Past**:
to describe an action that happened:	
a in the past but the time is not mentioned,	at a definite time in the past,
■ *I have seen that film.*	■ *I saw that film in October.*
b within an unfinished period of time,	within a finished period of time,
■ *I've seen him twice today.*	■ *I saw him twice last week.*
c in the past but is related to the present.	at some point in the past, even if the time is not mentioned.
■ *I've cut my hand and it hurts.*	■ *Columbus discovered America.*

Note that in "*Columbus discovered America*" the time is not mentioned but it is (or should be) known from history.

Decide whether the underlined verbs are right or wrong. Correct the mistakes.

1. Look at Teresa! She's dyed her hair.

   _____

2. I went to the States several times.

   _____

3. She washed the dishes and she is now having a rest.

   _____

4. When have you broken your arm?

   _____

5. Vangelis has composed the music for the film *Christopher Colombus*.

   _____

Exercise 1

For questions 1 - 9, read the text below and look carefully at each line. Some of the lines are correct, and some have a word which should not be there. If a line is correct, put a tick (✓) by the number. If a line has a word that should not be there, write the word next to the number.

WATER WORKS

1	You will have probably heard it people say that you should drink eight glasses of
2	water a day if you would want to stay healthy. Have you ever wondered why?
3	According to experts, the average person loses 10 cups of water a day: two
4	through sweating, two through breathing it and six through waste removal
5	(going to the toilet). You can replace up till to two cups through the food you
6	eat but the other eight cups must be replaced by drinking liquids, mainly water.
7	Eight cups is not enough, though, if you make exercise. The more you exercise,
8	the more water you need, not only to keep off your body temperature down and to
9	carry oxygen to your cells but also to protect joints and organs. So, how much water
	did you drink yesterday?

Exercise 2

For questions 10 - 16, read the text below. Use the word given in capitals at the end of each line to form a word that fits in the space in the same line.

NO LONGER A VICTIM

Almost a year ago Roberta Haycock was a **(10)** .... bystander during a bank **(11)** ....   HELP / ROB

Luckily, no one was hurt during the crime and Roberta, though shaken, was willing to forget the incident. She had

never considered the need to protect herself. However, her outlook on self-defence changed **(13)** ....   DRAMA

after a recent **(12)** .... outside her local supermarket. 'I have always been pretty indifferent about my   MUG

personal **(14)** .... ,' she says, 'but not any more.' Since her attack, Roberta has started self-defence   SAFE

classes and is working on a video called *'Not an Easy Target.'* In view of previous experiences, she stresses that

you shouldn't wait to become a victim before you start taking **(15)** ....   ACT

'Many people have the "it'll never happen to me" attitude,' she says,'but the risks are far greater than you might

think. For example a **(16)** .... occurs nearly every minute somewhere in the country. So do something   BURGLE

about it now. The next time a crime takes place make sure you are not just a bystander or, worse, the victim.'

Exercise 3

For questions 17 - 23, read the text again and think of the word which fits each space. Use only one word in each space.

NEOLITHIC EXHIBITION IN ATHENS, GREECE

The museum of Cycladic Art in Athens **(17)** .... organised the first exhibition ever devoted solely to relics from **(18)** .... Neolithic Age. Between 6800 BC and 3200 BC, early humans began to form permanent communities and built the cultural foundation for the civilisations that would follow.

The museum has **(19)** .... to gather nearly 400 items from Neolithic Greece from 52 Greek and Cypriot museums. The objects, some of which have **(20)** .... been shown, were all excavated during this century from hundreds of settlements, farms and cemeteries across Greece. The pieces include stone tools, pottery, jewellery and clay and marble figurines. Perhaps the **(21)** .... fascinating exhibit of all is the reconstruction of a prehistoric grave complete **(22)** .... skeleton. The grave was first discovered near a town **(23)** .... central Greece.

Exercise 4

For questions 24 - 28, complete the second sentence so that it has a similar meaning to the first sentence, using the word given. Do not change the word given.

24 Ken and Sandra are at the museum.	have
Both .... the museum.	
25 The government should provide more facilities so that disabled people can lead normal lives.	the
The government should provide more facilities so that .... can lead normal lives.	
26 William O'Brian has been accused of murdering his neighbour.	charged
William O'Brian .... murdering his neighbour.	
27 Nick has lived in London for a year.	since
Nick has .... year.	
28 Someone stole some money from my safe last night.	robbed
Someone .... some money last night.	

Personal Pronouns, Possessive Adjectives / Pronouns

Subject Pronouns	I	you	he	she	it	we	they
Object Pronouns	me	you	him	her	it	us	them
Possessive Adjectives	my	your	his	her	its	our	their
Possessive Pronouns	mine	yours	his	hers	its	ours	theirs

Personal Pronouns are used instead of nouns, proper nouns or noun phrases.

Subject Pronouns come **before** the verb.
  ■ *He passed the exam with a high mark.*

Object Pronouns come **after** the verb or after a preposition. ■ *Have you heard from him lately?*
  ■ *I told him the truth.*

Both **Possessive Pronouns** and **Possessive Adjectives** show that something belongs to someone.

Possessive Adjectives are followed by a noun.
  ■ *Where's my book?*

Possessive Pronouns are never followed by a noun.
  ■ *That sweater can't be yours.*

LEARNING TIPS	That is *my* book. A possessive
Remember that a possessive adjective is used in front of a noun:	pronoun is used alone, without a noun after it: That bicycle is *mine*.

Replace the <u>underlined</u> nouns with the appropriate pronouns.

1 'What's in that bag?' 'It's <u>Catherine's</u> new skirt.'

_____

2 A friend of <u>my father's</u> came to visit us yesterday.

_____

3 <u>John</u> has lied to <u>Mary</u>.

_____

4 I want <u>Helen</u> to give <u>the books</u> to John.

_____

5 Why are you laughing at <u>Peter</u>?

_____

6 Could you please put that down? It's <u>Mary's</u> and <u>Thomas'</u>.

_____

7 What time are <u>your parents</u> arriving from Leeds?

_____

some, any, no, every

Some and **any** mean a certain amount of or a certain number of. Both are used with either countable or uncountable nouns.

Some is mainly used in affirmative sentences.
  ■ *I can lend you some money.*
  It may be used in questions that are offers or requests when you expect an affirmative answer.
  ■ *Will you have some tea?*
  ■ *Can you lend me some money?*

Any is particularly used in negative and interrogative sentences.
  ■ *Are there any questions?*
  ■ *We didn't ask any questions.*
  It may be used in affirmative sentences meaning that it doesn't matter which person or thing is involved.
  ■ *You can find it in any supermarket.*

No means not any. It takes an affirmative verb to express a negative idea and vice versa.
  ■ *There were no problems with the new machine.*
  ■ *She was no help at all!*

Every means all persons or things involved. It is followed by a singular noun and therefore takes a singular verb.
  ■ *Every student in the classroom was pleased with the new teacher.*

Fill in the gaps with **some**, **any**, **no** or **every**.

1 Is there _____ bread left or should I go out and buy some?

2 There was _____ right answer to the question.

3 _____ bedroom in his mansion has its own bathroom.

4 There weren't _____ particularly difficult words in the passage.

5 Would you like _____ help with the washing up?

6 I'm free next week so we can meet _____ day you like.

7 Why didn't you ask me for _____ extra sheets of paper?

8 _____ student in the school has his own locker.

be going to vs. will

Use the form **be going + to - infinitive:**

i. to express sb's intention to do something
■ *I'm going to discuss it with him soon.*

ii. to make a prediction which is based on evidence
■ *I think it's going to rain. Look at all those black clouds!*

Use **will + infinitive without 'to':**

i. to express an intention or decision made at the moment of speaking
■ *I forgot all about fixing your bike but I'll do it right now.*

ii. to make predictions, threats, promises, offers, and requests
■ *If anybody moves, I'll shoot.*

Decide whether the underlined verbs are right or wrong. Correct the mistakes.

1. It's definite. <u>We will have</u> a baby!

_____

2. 'I'm hungry.' '<u>I'm going to make</u> you a sandwich.'

_____

3. 'One day <u>you were going to be</u> rich,' the fortune-teller told him.

_____

4. <u>I will buy</u> bread, cheese, and fruit. Do you need anything else?

_____

5. 'Oh dear! We haven't got any eggs left.'
'Don't worry. <u>I'm going to go</u> to the supermarket for you.'

_____

so, too, neither / nor, either

To avoid repeating an **affirmative statement** with a different subject, we can use:
so + auxiliary verb + subject:
■ *'John has gone away for the weekend.'*
'So has Mary.'

or **subject + auxiliary verb + too**
■ *My brother will help you if you like and I will too.*

To avoid repeating a **negative statement** with a different subject, we can use **neither/nor + auxiliary verb** in the affirmative + **subject:**
■ *I can't swim and neither/nor can Mary.*

or **subject + auxiliary verb** in the negative + **either:**
■ *He doesn't work very hard and his sister doesn't either.*

Respond to the statements by using <u>so</u>, <u>too</u>, <u>neither</u>, <u>nor</u>, <u>either</u>. Try to vary your responses.

1. George can't speak Chinese.

_____

2. They love classical music.

_____

3. We don't have to wear a uniform.

_____

4. I started school when I was six.

_____

5. Mary hasn't been to Japan.

_____

6. I'll help John if he wants me to.

_____

7. I have never eaten bird's nest soup.

_____

Unit 5

Exercise 1

For questions 1 - 12, read the text below and look carefully at each line. Some of the lines are correct, and some have a word which should not be there. If a line is correct, put a tick (✓) by the number. If a line has a word that should not be there, write the word next to the number.

LEAVE YOUR FRIEND AT HOME

1	For us our boys, a perfect Saturday night out isn't hanging out with our
2	mates but been having a date lined up with a girl who has submitted to our
3	charms. However, there is one thing that is sure to destroy all that lovely
4	anticipation - when you will arrive to see that your date has brought
5	company, in the shape of her best friend. You hope that your date's friend is
6	on her way somewhere else but goes deep down, you know exactly what
7	your date is going to say the next. 'I hope you don't mind,' she'll cheerily
8	explain. 'Susan was at a loose end!' Your romantic evening will be soon
9	turn into a night of polite chit-chat. What girls don't understand is that why it's
10	frightening enough entertaining one girl but when she brings her best friend
12	along, suddenly the whole evening it becomes a nightmare! What girls
12	should know is that three some is definitely a crowd.

Exercise 2

For questions 13 - 20, read the text below. Use the word given in capitals at the end of each line to form a word that fits in the space in the same line.

SWISS TIME SINCE 1899

At a time when digital instruments (13) .... monitor flight data at	ROUTINE
(14) .... speeds far above the earth, why continue improving	BELIEVE
(15) .... chronographs?	MECHANIC
(16) .... because there's more to time than technology.	PRECISE
Just ask Swiss Time, the world's (17) .... maker of time	LEAD
instruments for aviation (18)	PROFESSION
Its (19) .... designed and lovingly hand-polished watchcases put	BEAUTY
(20) .... progress in a broader, more rewarding perspective.	TECHNOLOGY

Exercise 3

For questions 21 - 29, read the text below and think of the word which fits each space. Use only one word in each space.

NEWS IN BRIEF

The proposal (21) .... include environment-awareness lessons (22) .... the school curriculum was a hot topic in Prime Minister's Question Time last week. Greenpeace representatives emphasized the need for lessons based (23) .... topics (24) .... as alternative energy, pollution control, and environmental protection to (25) .... taught in primary schools as a separate school subject. (26) .... to Colin Hull, Greenpeace Director of Educational Matters, 'Children are our future and it is (27) .... who are going to have to deal (28) .... the damage their parents and ancestors did to the planet so we have to teach them (29) .... to prevent further destruction of the earth and its natural resources.' The Minister of Education said that this would be an issue for further discussion.

Exercise 4

For questions 30 - 34, complete the second sentence so that it has a similar meaning to the first sentence, using the word given. Do not change the word given.

30 'I haven't studied for the Maths test today.' 'Neither have I.'	**either**
'I haven't studied for the Maths test today.' '..,'	
31 He claims that no detail has been left out.	**every**
He claims that .... included.	
32 These lecture notes are mine, not his.	**belong**
These lecture notes .... him.	
33 'I won't be in the office tomorrow. I'm going to see my mother in Bristol,' Marion said.	**because**
Marion said she wouldn't be in the office .... going to see her mother in Bristol.	
34 'You can't find a copy of the speech at just any library', she said.	**some**
You can only find a copy of the speech ...., she said.	

Phrasal verbs

take after
  resemble a member of one's family
take...away
  subtract; remove
take...in
  i. be able to understand
  ii. deceive
take off
  (of aircraft) leave the ground
take...on
  accept responsibility
take...over
  gain control of
take to
  have a liking for
take...up
  adopt a hobby

Fill in the gaps with the appropriate phrasal verb in the correct tense.

1 He soon _____ his teacher.

2 Don't _____ so much extra work.

3 He _____ his father more than his mother.

4 We were all _____ by his innocent looking face.

5 That looks disgusting. _____ it _____!

6 _____ swimming has relieved my back pain.

7 The plane will soon _____.

8 The trainee couldn't _____ all the information he was given.

9 Our company _____ by a multi-national.

Reflexive and Reciprocal pronouns

Reflexive or emphatic pronouns:
  **myself   yourself   himself   herself   itself
  ourselves   yourselves   themselves   oneself**
are used:
i. as objects after the verb when the subject and the object are the same,
  ■ *He cut himself with a knife.*
ii. to emphasize the subject or object,
  ■ *The manager himself came to the factory to talk to the workers.*
  ■ *The workers talked to the manager himself.*
iii. in the expressions: by himself = alone without company or help; for himself = in person, personally.
  ■ *She was angry because she had to do all the housework by herself.*
  ■ *If you don't believe me, come and see for yourself.*

Reciprocal pronouns: each other and **one another**, which are interchangeable, are used:
i. when two or more people / things do the same thing or share the same feelings,
  ■ *They are proud of each other.*
  ■ *The two cars collided with one another.*
ii. only as the object of the verb or preposition.
  ■ *They fought one another for hours.*
  ■ *They know each other quite well.*

Complete the sentences with either a reflexive or a reciprocal pronoun.

1 He cut _____ while he was trying to open a tin of beans.

2 Keith and Helen went to Disneyland and really enjoyed _____

3 We just stood there looking at _____ not knowing what to do.

4 She admired _____ in the mirror.

5 I wanted to see for _____ where the accident had happened

6 It is fully automatic. It can switch _____ on and off.

7 The little girl was proud she had tidied the room by _____.

8 The two dogs stared at _____ for some seconds before they attacked.

9 You can't go out looking like that. Just take a look at _____

10 Paula and Harry are madly in love with _____ and plan to ge married soon.

little, much, few, many, a lot of, plenty of

Little and **much** are used with uncountable nouns.

(Very) little means *hardly any* or *not much*.
- *He has little knowledge of computers.*

A little refers to a [small amount / quantity / length]
- *He has a little money left.*

Much refers to [a large amount / quantity]
- *Don't eat too much.*
- *She didn't say much about it.*

Few and **many** are used with countable nouns.

(Very) few means *hardly any* or *not many*.
- *Few students knew the answer.*

A few refers to [a small number]
- *There are a few magazines about hi-fi equipment.*

Many refers to [a large number]
- *The fall of the government was the result of many strikes.*

A lot of and **plenty of** are used with both countable and uncountable nouns.

A lot of refers to [a large amount] of sth or [a number of things]
- *The firm received a lot of orders for the new product.*
- *He had a lot of experience in the field.*

Plenty of means *a large amount/number* and it indicates that there is enough of something or there is more than needed
- *She's got plenty of money.*
- *There are always plenty of jobs to be done.*

Note: much and **many** are often used in negative sentences, esp. in spoken English, whereas **a lot of** and **plenty of** are often used in affirmative sentences.

Fill in the gaps using the words in bold on the left.

1. Don't worry, we've got _____ time to discuss it.

2. The waiting room was crowded because there were _____ students waiting to see the headmaster.

3. Only _____ people managed to survive the shipwreck.

4. Although she's told her brother _____ lies, he still loves her.

5. Unfortunately, I don't have _____ money left in my account.

6. Would you like _____ help?

7. He's got _____ good ideas. Perhaps we should listen to him.

8. How _____ people did you say were coming to the wedding?

9. There was _____ we could do to help the wounded soldier.

10. I don't know _____ shops where you could find something like that.

11. _____ men throughout history have shown such courage in the face of war.

12. I'm sure we'll find something on the subject. After all, there are _____ books to choose from.

Present Continuous vs. Present Simple for future actions

The **Present Continuous** and the **Present Simple** can be used to express future actions.

The **Present Continuous** is used for a definite arrangement in the near future. It is particularly used with verbs of movement such as *go, leave, come*.
- *He's leaving for Brussels next week.*

The **Present Simple** is used for a future action which is part of a timetable.
- *Schools open in early September.*
- *My train leaves at 4:30.*

Study the examples and see whether the <u>Present Continuous</u> or <u>Present Simple</u> have been used correctly.

1. What time is his plane landing?

_____

2. I visit my grandmother next weekend.

_____

3. The match starts at 4 o'clock in the afternoon.

_____

4. I meet my brother for lunch later this evening.

_____

5. She is finishing her studies in June.

_____

Unit 6

Exercise 1

For questions 1 - 9, read the text below and look carefully at each line. Some of the lines are correct, and some have a word which should not be there. If a line is correct, put a tick (✓) by the number. If a line has a word that should not be there, write the word next to the number.

VISITOR'S LONDON

1	The London Dungeon is the world-famous horror museum which set in the	
2	huge dark cellars in the Tooley Street, beneath London Bridge station.	
3	Based on historical facts, it presents a series of life-size and all too lifelike scenes	
4	are representing superstition, torture, and death in spine-chilling detail. Eerie	
5	sound effects and dramatic lighting create an excitingly	
6	macabre atmosphere from the moment visitors step themselves through the	
7	Dungeon doors. Next week will sees the opening of The Jack the Ripper	
8	Experience - where you can to take a walk through 19th century East End	
9	London and attempt to solve out this age-old murder mystery. However, if	
	you regard yourself as a nervous person at all, enter at your own risk.	

Exercise 2

For questions 10 - 17, read the text below. Use the word given in capitals at the end of each line to form a word that fits in the space in the same line.

WOLVES WATER DOWN ACCIDENTS

Sweden exports a lot of things but wolf urine must be on the way to becoming its

(10) .... export. The Swedes claim that a little wolf urine sprinkled over   **STRANGE**

roads can stop wild animals from crossing. This idea is based on research done at the

University of Umea, which used wolf urine to prevent deer from (11) ....   **COLLIDE**

with cars. During the 1994 Winter Olympic Games in Lellehammer, Norway, the method

was used to stop deer from crossing mountain roads.

Traffic officials in Kuwait are thinking of using the Swedish (12) .... to   **DISCOVER**

prevent camels (13) .... into cars. However, will the same thing work   **CRASH**

with camels? Swedish (14) .... Rune Petterson carried out many tests   **SEARCH**

with camels and the results show that it will.

Exercise 3

For questions 15 - 21, read the text below and think of the word which fits each space. Use only one word in each space.

ALLERGY ATTACK

When you finally manage to leave the city for fresh air and sunshine, does the inside of your mouth itch and your nose run like a tap? If **(15)** .... , welcome to the world of hay fever.

Hay fever is the common name for an allergic reaction caused by plant pollen floating in the air. The allergic reaction begins **(16)** .... an unfamiliar type of pollen lands in a person's nasal passage and sends the body's immune system into chaos.

So what can a sufferer do? Until recently, the answer was not **(18)** .... The only way to protect **(17)** .... was to stay indoors. But since very **(19)** .... people can stay under lock and key from spring to autumn, a better idea is to take antihistamines. However, many antihistamines cause sleepiness and if you have a **(20)** .... that involves operating machinery or driving, they should be avoided.

The only permanent solution is to see an allergist and start a series of desensitising injections. Although no one knows why they work, a **(21)** .... of people have reported a great reduction in their hay fever symptoms after two years of receiving allergy shots.

Exercise 4

For questions 22 - 26, complete the second sentence so that it has a similar meaning to the first sentence, using the word given. Do not change the word given.

22 There aren't many job opportunities in that field of work. There .... job opportunities in that field of work.		**few**
23 Both Albert and I are of the opinion that the company should give all its employees a bonus at Christmas. 'I honestly think that all the employees should get a Christmas bonus every year.' '... , too,' added Albert.		**believe**
24 I've got a few pounds I could lend you till you get your wages. I've got a .... I could lend you till you get your wages.		**money**
25 And how many more little jobs have you got to do before we can leave? And how .... have you got to do before we can leave?		**work**
26 They are so selfish; they don't care about their parents. They only .... ; they don't care about their parents.		**think**

Unit 7

Phrasal verbs

cut down on
    reduce (e.g. expenses, consumption)
cut in
        interrupt sb when speaking
cut...off
    i. disconnect when on the phone
    ii. (of supplies, communication)
        stop the flow
cut...out
    i. remove by cutting
    ii. stop eating a particular food
cut...up
    cut into pieces with a knife, etc

Fill in the gaps with the appropriate phrasal verb.

1. Why has the water supply been _____?

2. You smoke too much. Try to _____ smoking.

3. _____ the onions and put them in the pan.

4. Don't _____ when I'm speaking.

5. _____ sweets if you want to lose weight.

6. I was telling you about my dog when we were _____.

7. Who's _____ these pictures?

Prepositions of time: at , in, on

at	with exact time	■ *at four fifteen*
	with points of time	■ *at noon*
	with festivals	■ *at Christmas*
	with mealtimes	■ *at breakfast*
	with age	■ *at the age of 14*
	in the expression *at this/that time*	

in	with months	■ *in June*
	with seasons	■ *in (the) spring*
	with years	■ *in 1976*
	with centuries	■ *in the seventeenth century*
	with parts of the day	■ *in the morning / afternoon / evening*
	with historic periods of time	■ *in the Renaissance*
	in the expressions *in a week's/month's/year's time*	

on with particular days and with parts of the day when the name of the day is also mentioned
    ■ *on Monday, on Thursday morning*
with parts of the day when they refer to the day itself
    ■ *on that morning, on a cold winter afternoon with dates*
    ■ *on the sixth of September 1991*

Use at, on, in to fill in the gaps.

1. He was visited by his lawyer _____ 23 May, 2002.

2. He said he would be here _____ your wedding anniversary.

3. My uncle only goes to church _____ Easter.

4. _____ this time of day, the traffic is quite heavy.

5. My grandfather was killed _____ the Second World War.

6. I enjoy doing the garden early _____ the morning.

7. Did you say the office opened _____ 8:30 or 9:00?

8. The house was built _____ the 1800s but has been recently renovated.

9. If everything goes well, you can have a couple of days off _____ the autumn.

10. I didn't sleep very well because somebody woke me up _____ the middle of the night.

11. Jake has some free time _____ Monday and Thursday afternoons.

12. The plane leaves _____ 7:00 o'clock _____ 15th July.

13. The building should be finished some time _____ May.

14. The family always gets together _____ dinner time.

The suffixes: -less and -ful

Many adjectives can be formed by adding the suffixes -less or -ful to nouns.

-less means that sb or sth lacks what the noun refers to:

- *This appliance is useless. (This appliance has no use.)*
- *He is a tireless worker. (He is a worker who never gets tired.)*

-ful means with or having the quality of:

- *This book is very useful. (This book has a use.)*
- *Green is a restful colour.*

Form adjectives by adding either -less or -ful to the nouns in capitals.

1 A baby is almost completely _____.

HELP

2 How can you be so _____ after everything I've done for you? **HEART**

3 Next time you do this exercise, try to be more _____. **CARE**

4 Why do you look so _____? Have you got something on your mind? **THOUGHT**

Past Perfect Simple vs. Past Perfect Continuous

Use the **Past Perfect Simple** (*I had done*) to refer to an action or event that occurred before a particular time in the past when the result of that past action is related to a specific time in the past.

- *John didn't go to the cinema with his friends because he had seen that film*
- *I had finished my work, so I could go out with them.*
- *His mother was angry because he hadn't finished his homework.*

The **Past Perfect Continuous** (*I had been doing*) is used to refer to an action that began before a point of reference in the past and continued up to that time or stopped just before it.

- *We had been waiting for over an hour before the plane finally took off.*
- *I was feeling tired. I had been working since seven that morning.*
- *He was happy when he met her at the party. He had been trying to approach her for months.*

Correct the mistakes.

1 When I arrived Mary left already.

_____

2 He fainted because he hasn't eaten anything for two days.

_____

3 I was asleep for two hours when I heard the telephone ringing.

_____

4 My mother was furious with me when I finally arrived because she was waiting for me for over three hours.

_____

5 I never flew before so I was really scared.

_____

feel, sound, taste, smell, look

The verbs **feel, sound, taste, smell**, and **look**, are usually followed by adjectives.

- *That cake you made tasted delicious.*
- *You sound exhausted. Why don't you have a rest?*
- *This material feels very soft.*
- *Doesn't she look beautiful?*
- *Don't these roses smell sweet?*

Fill in the gaps with appropriate adjectives.

1 How much money did you pay for this perfume? It smells _____.

2 This silk shirt feels _____ .

3 He sounded _____ on the phone.

4 Sea water tastes _____.

5 You look _____ . Have you been jogging?

Exercise 1

For questions 1 - 9, read the text below and look carefully at each line. Some of the lines are correct, and some have a word which should not be there. If a line is correct, put a tick (✓) by the number. If a line has a word that should not be there, write the word next to the number.

DIRTY DISHES

1 George called his mother and announced him excitedly that he had just

2 been met the woman of his dreams but he didn't know what to do next. His

3 mother suggested that he send to her flowers and invite his new friend to

4 his apartment for a home cooked meal. George thought this a great

5 strategy and in a week later, the woman came to dinner. His mother phoned

6 after their date to see how things had gone on.

7 'I was totally humiliated,' he moaned. 'She insisted on washing the dishes.'

8 'What's wrong with that?' asked from his mother.

9 'We hadn't started to eating yet,' George replied.

Exercise 2

For questions 10 - 20, read the text below. Use the word given in capitals at the end of each line to form a word that fits in the space in the same line.

THE UNWANTED GUEST

(10) .... placing the rifle he had carried on his shoulder in a corner of — CARE

the room, he advanced to the (11) .... , and without speaking, or even — FIRE

glancing at me, (12) .... lit his pipe and began smoking. — THINK

The dogs, after growling and snapping at the (13) .... cat, gave me a — PITY

very (14) .... reception. They sat down on the hearthstone on either — POLITE

side of their (15) .... master, (16) .... observing all — SILENCE/OBEY

that he did.

There was a (17) .... difference between the dogs. One was a bulldog — REMARK

of the largest size (18) .... , an impressive and (19) .... — IMAGINE/POWER

brute; the other was small, deep-chested, and strong-limbed. I watched the man and his

companions with silent (20) .... — CURIOUS

EXERCISE 3

For questions 21 - 28, read the text below and think of the word which fits each space. Use only one word in each space.

BIG FOOT

It was the end of February. A couple were sitting in their car one night, just gazing (21) .... the stars above when they saw an unexpected sight in the beam of their car's headlights. It had (22) .... stopped raining and there was no wind. They stopped looking at the stars and immediately lowered (23) .... eyes to the front of the car. That's when they (24) .... it. Both of them stared at it until it was (25) .... of sight. (26) .... a few seconds, it had crossed the road in only three or four steps. They wondered (27) .... it was a horse or a cow, but it was too tall. When they reported their sighting to the authorities, they described it as being 3 or 4 metres tall and that they had never seen (28) .... like it before.

EXERCISE 4

For questions 29 - 33, complete the second sentence so that it has a similar meaning to the first sentence, using the word given. Do not change the word given.

29 Peter had been caught peeping through the keyhole, so he was punished.	**as**
Peter .... caught peeping through the keyhole.	
30 There's no point in advising him. He won't listen.	**pointless**
It's .... He won't listen.	
31 She tried to peer through the fog but she couldn't see the car in the distance.	**make**
She tried to peer through the fog .... the car in the distance.	
32 I glimpsed him in the crowd just before he disappeared from sight.	**caught**
I .... in the crowd just before he disappeared from sight.	
33 The food smelled good and it tasted delicious too.	**only**
Not .... good, but it tasted delicious too.	

Unit 8

Phrasal verbs

break down

  i. (of a machine, engine, etc) stop working

  ii. collapse emotionally or physically

break in(to)

  enter a building illegally or by force

break...off

  (of talks, agreements, etc) end, terminate

break out

  i. (of war, disease, etc) begin suddenly

  ii. escape from prison

break up

  end a relationship

Fill in the gaps with the appropriate phrasal verb in the correct tense.

1 They've _____ peace talks between the two warring countries.

2 She _____ and cried when she heard the bad news.

3 When we returned, we found that our house had been _____.

4 A group of political prisoners _____ late last night.

5 Their marriage seems to be _____.

6 The epidemic that _____ recently has claimed hundreds of lives.

7 We'll have to use the stairs as the lift has _____.

Prepositions of place: at, in, on

at: to talk about a specific point in space where sth is found ■ *at the door*

-to talk about public places or institutions ■ *at the gallery*

-to say that sb is at an event ■ *at the party / football match*

-in the expressions: *at home, at work, at the end, at the front, at the top, at the back,* and also: *at war, at rest*

in: to talk about a place as an area ■ *in a country/town/village* to talk about sth or sb that is within clearly defined limits ■ *in a building / box*

Compare:

at the cinema   *He's at the cinema.* (=He's watching the film.)
in the cinema   *He's in the cinema.* (=He's in the building but not necessarily watching the film.)

at 15 Daisy Ave.   (when the house number is given)
in/on Daisy Ave.   (when only the name of the street is given)
at / on the corner of a street
in the corner of a room

on: to talk about sb or sth touching or covering the surface of an object ■ *on the table* to talk about an area of land (not the precise position) where sth is or happens ■ *She works on a farm / on a building site.* to say that sth or sb is in a public vehicle

■ *on the bus, on the train*

and in the expressions:

■ *on the river, on the road, on the coast*

Use **at, in, on** to fill in the gaps.

1 He was relaxing _____ the sofa in front of the fire.

2 The sweet shop _____ the corner of West Street and Bank Avenue sells Swiss chocolate.

3 They were drinking coffee _____ a little cafe _____ Brady Street.

4 She has bought a beautiful little cottage _____ the river.

5 Fred was _____ the bus when the accident happened.

6 I didn't manage to see the Manager because he was _____ a conference.

7 I've left my keys _____ home _____ the kitchen.

8 I'll meet you back _____ the hotel.

9 Would you mind putting these things away _____ the drawer for me?

10 Ms Hanson is waiting for you _____ your office, sir.

11 If you keep on talking, I'll have to make you sit _____ the front of the class.

12 I remember doing that when I was _____ school.

Adverbs of manner

Most **adverbs of manner** are formed by adding **-ly** to the corresponding adjective. But adjectives ending in:

-y, change **-y** to **-i** before taking **-ly,**
- *pretty - prettily*

-able or **-ible**, change to **-ably** or **-ibly** to form **adverbs,**
- *probable - probably, terrible - terribly*

-ly have no corresponding adverb forms (with the exception of *early* and *kindly* which are the same in both forms). Some of these adjectives are *lovely, brotherly, fatherly, friendly.*

To express manner with these adjectives, use adverb phrases with **way** or **manner**.
- *in a lovely way, in a friendly manner*

Remember the exceptions: good - well, hard - hard, fast - fast.

Complete the sentences with the adverb of the word in capitals.

1. You should try to behave _____.
RESPONSIBLE

2. Peter is studying _____ for his exam.
HARD

3. She was sitting _____ in the armchair watching her favourite TV programme.
COMFORTABLE

4. George was playing _____ in the garden. HAPPY

5. She dances very _____ for her age.
GOOD

The Gerund

The **gerund** always ends in **-ing** and is a noun formed from a verb which expresses an action or state. It can be used in the same way as any other noun.

subject **Smoking** is bad for your health.
object I hope you don't mind my **smoking**.
complement The worst thing for your stomach is **eating** before you go to bed.
adjective An **eating** apple is far sweeter than a cooking apple.
after a Why don't you have a rest after
preposition **exercising**?

Certain verbs and expressions are followed by the gerund

LEARNING TIPS
Remember that when the *gerund* is the subject of the sentence, the verb is *singular.*

Put the words in the right order to make sentences.

1. Jane / stick / to / walking / a / use / has.
_____

2. a / potatoes / gadget / bought / I / special / peeling / for / have.
_____

3. the / many / in / eyes / for / front / of / so / spending / TV / your / is / hours / bad.
_____

4. most / washing up / is / hate / what / I.
_____

like, love, hate, prefer

The verbs **like, love, hate, prefer** are followed by:

i. the **gerund** when they express general likes, dislikes or preferences.
- *I hate working on my own.*
- *She has never liked exercising.*

ii. the **to - infinitive** when they are used after **would** or when they refer to a particular case.
- *I would prefer to go in my own car.*
- *We would love to help you out.*

Match 1-5 with A-E to complete the sentences.

1. I'd really love
2. Would you like
3. John hates
4. I prefer
5. I hate

A to think that my holidays are over.
B visiting friends to staying at home.
C going to parties. He finds them boring.
D to go for a walk.
E me to repeat the question?

33

Unit 8

Exercise 1

For questions 1 - 14, read the text below and look carefully at each line. Some of the lines are correct, and some have a word which should not be there. If a line is correct, put a tick (✓) by the number. If a line has a word that should not be there, write the word next to the number.

NOT THE BEST OF FRIENDS

1	Travel is a remarkable thing. Put down two perfect strangers side by side in	
2	an unfamiliar environment and what happens? More often than not they	
3	start to chatting, exchanging confidences, sharing experiences and before	
4	you can know it they're instant best friends. It could happen anywhere, on a	
5	boat, in a train or at a corner cafe in some foreign city; when the common	
6	factor is travel with all its accompanying excitements of new places, new	
7	experiences, new people. It's only for much later, after cards have been	
8	exchanged, addresses have been carefully written in filofaxes when they're	
9	nearly home and how their real best friends are there to meet them that reality	
10	bites. All the things those two strangers had better in common, such as both	
11	being human beings, maybe from the same country, even the same city	
12	don't seem to be very important enough to turn acquaintances into soul	
13	mates. If a holiday friend actually took up a careless invitation to pay visit	
14	whenever they were in the near neighbourhood, the other holiday friend	
	would most probably run as fast as he could.	

Exercise 2

For questions 15 - 21, read the text below. Use the word given in capitals at the end of each line to form a word that fits in the space in the same line.

SHOPPING ON THE EMERALD ISLE

Tradition is more than (15) .... when you look in the shop windows of — EVIDENCE

Ireland. The chance to buy high-quality handcrafts made with the finest Irish materials

should (16) .... not be missed. Prices are (17) .... — ABSOLUTE/ORDINARY

modest. Tweed from Donegal is among the best (18) .... cloth in — WOOL

the world. From the other end of the country comes the unequalled quality glassware

and crystal of Waterford. Limerick craftswomen still make some of the world's

(19) .... lace. Gold and silversmiths following age-old customs of Celtic — LOVELY

design and workmanship produce superb and unusual (20) .... All are — JEWEL

very Irish and bear the (21) .... stamp of style, excellence and expertise. — MISTAKE

Exercise 3

For questions 22 - 31, read the text below and think of the word which fits each space. Use only one word in each space.

MOBILE MANIA

Initially, mobile phones were used almost exclusively by business executives who needed to be contacted for important messages or critical business meetings. Today, with lower subscription costs, cellular communication has turned (22) .... a mobile mania. You'll see teenagers chatting happily with their friends (23) .... school, in clubs or (24) .... buses. Parents and their children (25) .... them so that the former can keep track of the latter and the elderly use them because it gives them a (26) .... of security. Cellular phones have become (27) .... popular that a German magazine has actually written an entire article on the proper way to use a mobile phone. Some of these rules include: (28) .... your mobile off at the opera because the people who are there have spent money to listen to voices other (29) .... yours, not using it on the bus because people are sure to think that you're trying to impress them, and most importantly, not lending your mobile to the wrong person. For instance, a problem (30) .... arise if a husband lends his phone to his wife and then his boss tries to reach him. (31) .... general, try not to be showy about it, because after all, everyone else has probably got one too.

Exercise 4

For questions 32 - 36, complete the second sentence so that it has a similar meaning to the first sentence, using the word given. Do not change the word given.

32 His English is very good. He speaks	well
33 An exciting way to see the world is to travel by boat. .... is an exciting way to see the world.	travelling
34 The museum would rather spend its money on works of art that may become priceless in the future. The museum .... its money on works of art that may become priceless in the future.	prefer
35 There's nothing she hates more than calculating the expense of each project. She hates calculating the expense of each project	anything
36 I hope you don't mind if I smoke. I hope you don't	my

Unit 9

Phrasal verbs

run across
  find or meet sb or sth
  (usually pleasant) unexpectedly
run after
  chase, pursue
run away
  move away quickly from a place
  or a person
run into
  i. meet unexpectedly
  ii. collide with
run out (of)
  have no more of sth left
run...over
  i. hit sb with a vehicle
  ii. examine quickly
run up against
  experience problems or difficulties unexpectedly

Fill in the gaps with the appropriate phrasal verb in the correct tense.

1 Guess who I _____ yesterday?
2 Let's _____ these figures again.
3 What made her _____ from home?
4 The project won't be completed as we have _____ serious difficulties.
5 At some point, I _____ patience and started shouting at him.
6 Stop _____ her. She's not worth it.
7 I _____ dear old Mrs Grainger in the supermarket today.
8 To avoid _____ the little boy, the driver crashed into a wall.
9 She was blinded by the sun and _____ a passing cab.

ago vs. before

Ago is used to refer to a certain time in the past which is measured back from the present.
  ■ *I went to London four years ago. (=I haven't been to London for four years / since 1999.)*

Note: **ago** is only used with verbs in the Simple Past or the Past Continuous.
  ■ *George must be here. He was parking the car five minutes ago.*

Before is used to refer to an earlier time or event in the past than that mentioned.
  ■ *Last year, I left the team that I had joined four years before.*

Use either _ago_ or _before_ to fill in the gaps.

1 Tom phoned only five minutes _____.
2 I'm sure I've met you _____.
3 The football match had started_____ Tom's phone call.
4 He lived in Lancaster ten years _____ when he was doing his postgraduate studies.
5 He got here at four but Jane had left fifteen minutes _____ then.

Suffixes: -able/-ible, -ian/-an

-able (also **-ible**) added to a verb forms adjectives meaning **able to be + past participle**.
  ■ *recognisable = able to be recognised*

-ian / -an added to nouns (often nouns of place) forms personal nouns or adjectives meaning *belonging to* or *pertaining to*.
  ■ *Athenian, Parisian, Elizabethan, republican*

Use the word given in capitals at the end of each line to form a word that fits in the space.

1 I'd like to speak to the person _____ for this project. **RESPONSE**
2 I'm afraid this isn't _____. You'll have to do it again. **ACCEPT**
3 The _____ was very helpful so it didn't take me long to find the book I needed. **LIBRARY**
4 I found his demands quite _____. **REASON**

36

Narrative Tenses

Here are the most common tenses used in narrative. These tenses may appear in any order in a story but remember:

The **Past Continuous** is used to set the scene by describing the events that were taking place at the beginning of the story.

The **Simple Past** is used to talk about actions or a sequence of events in the story.

The **Past Perfect** is used to describe events that happened before the actual story begins.

> ■ *It was raining and the house was cold and lonely. Celia walked over to the desk and picked up the letter.*
> *It was the letter that Bill had sent to her earlier that morning saying that he was leaving her.*

Use the appropriate tense of the verb in brackets to fill in the gaps.

When I **(1)**_____ (leave) home it **(2)**_____ (get) cloudy. I **(3)**_____ (start) walking quickly along the street because I **(4)**_____ (wake up) late that morning. A couple of kids **(5)**_____ (play) noisily next to my house and drivers **(6)**_____ (blow) their horns. Suddenly, I **(7)**_____ (hear) the sound of two cars crashing into each other. I **(8)**_____ (stop) and **(9)**_____ (look) around. I **(10)**_____ (turn) and **(11)**_____ (see) the two drivers who **(12)**_____ (collide) with each other staring at a little cat as it happily **(13)**_____ (cross) the road.

used to, would, be / get used to

Used + to infinitive is used to express a habitual past action or a past situation which is no longer true, or contrasts with the present situation.

> ■ *I used to play tennis a lot but I don't have the time now.*

Questions and negatives are formed with **did**.

> ■ *Didn't he use to go fishing every day?*

Would + infinitive without 'to' may replace **used + to-infinitive** when it is an action verb.

> ■ *I would go to the cinema at least once a week when I was a student.*

Be / get used to + gerund / noun / pronoun means *be/become accustomed to.*

> ■ *You'll soon get used to the noise in this neighbourhood.*

> ■ *Julie is used to waking up early, so she doesn't mind taking the six o'clock train.*

Rephrase these sentences using used to / would or be / get used to.

❶ John smoked a lot in the past but he has now given up smoking.

John _____

❷ My son doesn't believe that storks bring new babies but he did once.

My son _____

❸ I can't wake up early in the morning. I'm not used to it.

I'm not _____

❹ She has gradually learned to work long hours.

She is now _____

❺ When Joanna was a child, she woke up late every morning.

As a child, Joanna _____

❻ When he came to India, he didn't like eating spicy food, but he soon became accustomed to it.

After living in India for some time, he _____

_____

Unit 9

Exercise 1

For questions 1 - 9, read the text below and look carefully at each line. Some of the lines are correct, and some have a word which should not be there. If a line is correct, put a tick (✓) by the number. If a line has a word that should not be there, write the word next to the number.

IT'S MAGIC

1	Before a few years ago, I decided to take a magic class because I was	
2	feeling down and needed to renew my sense of fun. It class turned out to be	
3	just the thing. Most of the tricks were pretty easy and the most best thing	
4	about the classes was that they were cheap. All the 'equipment' I needed it	
5	was a pen, a few rubber bands, and some string. Within a few days, I had	
6	got become familiar with such exotic tricks as Mental Mover (in which a pen	
7	moves up a rubber band) and Professor's Nightmare (connecting three	
8	ropes into one without knots). If I had wanted an audience, I would use my	
9	cats. They used to watch carefully but couldn't work out the secrets - unlike	

my husband. I still keep two rubber bands in the bathroom drawer, and I
practise some of my tricks while I'm getting ready for work.

Exercise 2

For questions 10 - 18, read the text below. Use the word given in capitals at the end of each line to form a word that fits in the space in the same line.

DRESSING UP

Costumes in films can range from Tarzan's simple loincloth to the dazzling, historically accurate,
(10) .... clothes worn in 'Orlando' (1993). Costumes today are the (11) ....   **ELIZABETH/**
of costume designers while a hundred years ago, in the early days of cinema, actors and   **CREATE**
(12) .... used to wear their own clothes or hire costumes from (13) ....   **ACT/THEATRE**
prop companies. One story goes that Charlie Chaplin created the costume of the *Tramp* by bor-
rowing items of clothing from other (14) .... at the Keystone studios. Later, the big   **COMEDY**
studios built up their own costume departments. When the 'talkies' arrived just before the end of
the 1920s, costumes suddenly presented (15) .... problems. The sensitive micro-   **EXPECT**
phones would pick up every rustle forcing costume makers to look for softer, silent fabrics. In
the golden age of Hollywood, costumes in (16) .... films were often more fantastic   **HISTORY**
than they were accurate. The (17) .... was on creating the right atmosphere rather   **EMPHASIZE**
than paying (18) .... to detail. Nowadays, great care is taken when creating period   **ATTEND**
clothes. Costume designers study paintings and books and have costumes hand-stitched so as
not to look too neat and modern.

Exercise 3

For questions 19 - 25, read the text below and think of the word which fits each space. Use only one word in each space.

HEART OF STONE

Paula pulled up outside the villa, turned (19) .... the engine and stepped out of the car. It took her a while to (20) .... accustomed to the darkness, but when she did, she made her way to the front door. She opened it as quietly as she could and quickly climbed up the wooden staircase. Over the past few weeks she had become so (21) .... with the layout of the house that she had no trouble (22) .... her way in the dark. She walked into the room that had been her office and quickly gathered together her sketches and plans. When she had first seen the house three weeks (23) .... , she had fallen in love with it. Now she needed to get away from it as quickly as (24) .... With bundles of blueprints under her arms, she ran down the stairs to the front door. As her hand turned the handle, the door burst open and Paula came face to face with the man she had been running (25) .... from.

Exercise 4

For questions 26 - 30, complete the second sentence so that it has a similar meaning to the first sentence, using the word given. Do not change the word given.

26 Waking up at six o'clock in the morning doesn't bother him any more.	used
He .... waking up at six o'clock in the morning.	
27 My uncle used to clean his bicycle every Sunday afternoon.	would
My uncle .... his bicycle every Sunday afternoon.	
28 Emma soon got used to living in London.	grew
Emma soon .... living in London.	
29 He was barely recognisable after his long illness.	could
He .... after his long illness.	
30 Don't worry. You'll soon find out how the machine works.	familiar
Don't worry. You'll soon .... this machine works.	

Unit 10

Phrasal verbs

pull...down
  demolish

pull in / up
  stop a vehicle

pull...off
  succeed in doing

pull out
  i. discontinue an activity or agreement
  ii. drive out of a place and into the road

pull up
  slow down and stop a vehicle

Fill in the gaps with the appropriate phrasal verb.

1 Check for any oncoming vehicles and _____ carefully.

2 A decision was taken to _____ the old factory.

3 _____ at the next corner, please.

4 He _____ at the rest spot to have a look at the wonderful view.

5 We've invested too much money and time to _____ of this deal now.

6 He was the only one capable of _____ that kind of stunt.

by, on, in

by + noun (without a / the / my) is used to refer to:

i. the type of transport we use,
  ■ *by bus, by car, by train*
ii. how we travel.
  ■ *by sea, by air, by land*

on + a / the / my + noun is used to refer to:
i. forms of travel such as trains, buses, coaches, boats, aeroplanes,
  ■ *on a plane, on the bus, on my boat*
ii. forms of transport that people ride.
  ■ *on a motorbike, on a camel*

Note: on foot means walking
in + a / the / my + noun is used to talk about vehicles used to travel (except: buses, coaches, bikes)
  ■ *in a taxi, in the aeroplane*

Some of the sentences below are incorrect. Correct the mistakes.

1 They all left in Tom's car.

_____

2 Last summer, he went to Germany on rail.

_____

3 In the past, people travelled in horseback.

_____

4 He arrived at the office by his motorbike.

_____

5 Why don't you go by ferry?

_____

6 The Prime Minister has never travelled in a bus.

_____

7 The school is so near we can go by foot.

_____

adjective or adverb?

Note that the following words can be used both as adjectives and adverbs with no change in their form.

fast   hard   late   early   right

straight well (= healthy)   wrong

■ *He drives fast.*   ■ *He's a fast driver.*

LEARNING TIPS

Remember that an adjective answers the question *"What kind?"* and an adverb answers the question *"How?"*

Fill in each gap with one of the adjectives or adverbs on the left. Say if it's an adjective or an adverb.

1. He was _____ for the interview and as a result didn't get the job.

2. 'It isn't _____ to tell lies,' my mother always used to say.

3. I don't feel _____. I'd better see a doctor.

4. 'Have I written it _____?' the little boy asked his teacher.

The Infinitive

I. The **to-infinitive** can be used:

i.   after certain verbs such as want, wish, like, etc
     ■ *She wants to go to a party.*

ii. after certain adjectives such as happy, pleased, disappointed, etc
     ■ *I'm sorry to tell you that you have failed the exam.*

iii. after impersonal expressions such as It's necessary / important / easy, etc
     ■ *It's difficult to go there at night.*
     ■ *It's important for him to know the truth.*

iv. to express purpose
     ■ *I went to the bank manager to ask for a loan.*

v.   after **too + adjective / adverb or adjective / adverb + enough**
     ■ *He thought he was too clever to deal with such minor issues.*
     ■ *He felt he was not experienced enough to handle it.*
     ■ *He arrived at the station too late to catch the train.*
     ■ *Mary studied hard enough to pass the exam.*

vi. as the subject of a sentence
     ■ *To err is human, to forgive divine.*

vii. after **something / anybody / nowhere**, etc and after question words such as **how, where**, etc
     ■ *I can't think of anything to say to him.*
     ■ *We had no idea where to look for him.*

II. Use the **infinitive without 'to'**:

i.   after modal verbs
     ■ *We can / may / might / could meet in the afternoon.*

ii. after certain verbs
     ■ *The kidnappers let him go free when they got the money.*

iii. after would rather.., had better....,Why?, and Why not...?
     ■ *I'd rather see a play than watch TV.*
     ■ *You'd better call back later.*
     ■ *Why stay indoors on a sunny day like today?*
     ■ *Why not spend the evening with friends?*

Use the to-infinitive or infinitive without 'to' to fill in the gaps.

1. Could you possibly _____ (type) these letters for me?

2. I'd rather _____ (stay) at home than _____ (go) out with you.

3. It's really good _____ (see) you again.

4. We had no idea where _____ (look) for him.

5. That dress is too formal _____ (wear) during the daytime.

6. I've decided _____ (tell) him the truth.

7. There's a basket _____ (put) your dirty laundry in.

8. _____ (admit) you've done something wrong takes a lot of courage.

9. 'I want you _____ (do) it now,' he said.

10. Our parents rarely let us _____ (watch) television on a school night.

11. You are going to have _____ (face) him sooner or later.

12. We'd better _____ (leave) before it gets dark.

13. Don't tell me you've nowhere _____ (go) on a Saturday night.

14. Why not _____ (go) to Austria for Christmas?

15. Is it necessary for both of you _____ (go)?

Unit 10

Exercise 1

For questions 1 - 12, read the text below and look carefully at each line. Some of the lines are correct, and some have a word which should not be there. If a line is correct, put a tick (✓) by the number. If a line has a word that should not be there, write the word next to the number.

1	'Did you remember to feed the goldfish?', 'Erm, sorry I forgot so. I've got a
2	lot on my mind, you know.' Nearly everyone has found by themselves in a
3	similar situation, giving off a similar excuse. But have you ever asked yourself
4	why we forget things when we have a lot on our minds? If we could to
5	remember our whole lives in as much detail as the last hour, how we would
6	become very confused. It is the process of 'fading' the immediate past
7	which it helps us to remember the sequence of events in our lives. Our
8	brains have a limited total capacity, so that the forgetting allows us to adapt
9	in any order to make room for new memories. The time of day also has a strong
10	influence on memory. Experiments testing people on things that they have
11	just been learnt show that short-term memory gets worse as the day progresses
12	on (probably due to increased tiredness). So the next time you forget to do
	something, or forget doing something it's because your memory just ran out of space.

Exercise 2

For questions 13 - 18, read the text below. Use the word given in capitals at the end of each line to form a word that fits in the space in the same line.

TRAVEL PAINS

Some years ago I (13) .... had to travel from London to Paris by plane. Of **REGULAR**
course, planes were often late and there were frequent delays. One day while we were wait-
ing to take off, an (14) .... told us to expect another lengthy wait. I noticed **ANNOUNCE**
a member of the crew at the front of the cabin, and because I wanted to pass the time, I
decided to go up to her and tell her about other problems I had had on this airline. She lis-
tened to me (15) .... 'Sir,' she finally asked, 'what's your name?' With **CARE**
images of free (16) .... and better (17) .... dancing in **FLY / SERVE**
my head, I pronounced my name clearly and spelled it for her. She nodded and repeated my
name to check if it was right. I couldn't help feeling (18) .... while waiting **PATIENCE**
for her reply. 'Well, Mr Reiman,' she said, 'I must remember to avoid any flights listing you
as a passenger.'

Exercise 3

For questions 19 - 25, read the text below and think of the word which fits each space. Use only one word in each space.

TRAVELLING CLEAN, TRAVELLING GREEN

Why are most big cities dirty, smelly places? Mainly because of cars. Every time you take a ride (19) .... a car, petrol is converted into a number of pollutants which are then pumped out of the exhaust pipe into the air. Of course, there is an alternative: using catalytic converters or other kinds of fuel. Even chicken manure will do the trick if the engine is adapted to take it! But that's still a long way off. Right now we should concentrate on what we already have. Public transport, for example. When travelling (20) .... bus, the same number of people can get (21) .... their destinations with fewer traffic jams, less pollution, and fewer accidents. What more could (22) .... ask for? For a start, a more efficient transport service. Unfortunately, it will take about 20 years for that to happen. Till then the only real 'green' alternatives are travelling (23) .... bike or (24) .... foot. Bicycles are clean, cheap, healthy and fun. But it is often too dangerous to ride a bike in the city and most people have forgotten how to use their legs. So, we (25) .... to get our city councils to create bicycle lanes and more areas for pedestrians.

Exercise 4

For questions 26 - 30, complete the second sentence so that it has a similar meaning to the first sentence, using the word given. Do not change the word given.

26 I'd prefer to go to Cuba by air than by sea.   **rather**
I .... to Cuba by air than by sea.

27 We'll be entering Henry in the race. He's the fastest runner we've got.   **runs**
We'll be entering Henry in the race. He .... anyone else we've got.

28 The baker's is only two stops away. Why don't you try walking there for a change?   **foot**
The baker's is only two stops away. Why don't you try .... for a change?

29 I'm sure I wrote the message down somewhere.   **remember**
I .... the message down somewhere.

30 I'm always late for work no matter what time I leave home.   **turn**
I .... for work no matter what time I leave home.

Unit 11

Phrasal verbs

bring...about
>   cause to happen

bring...back
>   return sth / sb; restore or reintroduce sth

bring...round
>   make conscious again

bring...up
>   raise (esp. a child or a particular subject)

Fill in the gaps with the appropriate phrasal verb.

1 The doctors managed to _____ him
_____ .

2 What has _____ all these changes?

3 I intend to _____ this matter
_____ with the board of directors.

4 The idea of _____ corporal
punishment to schools is outrageous.

5 _____ children is one the most difficult
things one can do.

6 Coming back here after so many years has _____
_____ lovely memories.

on, onto, over, above, on (the) top of

on:
touching, fixed to, covering the upper or outer side
>   ■ *The cat was lying happily on my bed.*

onto:
showing movement or position on; usually used to say where someone or something falls or is put
>   ■ *My dog jumped onto the bed to have a nap.*

over:
directly above; higher than but not touching; covering
>   ■ *Hang that picture over the fireplace.*

above:
in a higher position than
>   ■ *They climbed up the mountain to a point of 2,000 feet above sea level.*

on (the) top of:
placed over, resting on
>   ■ *Put your book on (the) top of the others on the desk.*

after vs. afterwards
After, as a preposition, is usually followed by a noun or pronoun.
>   ■ *Why don't we meet after dinner?*

Afterwards is an adverb meaning: *after that*.
>   ■ *We had dinner and went home afterwards.*

Use on, onto, over, above, on (the) top of, after or afterwards to fill in the gaps.

1 'Where shall I put the luggage trolley?' 'Put it _____
the wardrobe.'

2 He kicked the ball _____ the wall and had to
go to the neighbours to ask for it.

3 I made the beds and did the washing up _____.

4 The cat climbed _____ the table to drink the milk.

5 They decided to go for a walk _____ dinner.

6 The sun had already risen high _____ the
horizon.

7 She couldn't reach the cupboards _____ her head.

8 Remember to leave the keys _____ the table.

9 It was an elegant apartment unlike the one _____ .

10 As he stepped _____ the platform, he tripped
and fell.

11 Let's get a bite to eat _____ the play.

12 Don't put the toys _____ that box over there.
It's got the X-mas decorations in it.

Comparatives, Superlatives

-er and **-est** are suffixes used to form comparatives and superlatives of:

i. monosyllabic adjectives,
- ■ *tall - taller - the tallest*

ii. adjectives of two syllables ending in **-er**, **-y**, **-ow** and **-ly**
- ■ *clever - cleverer - the cleverest*
- ■ *happy - happier - the happiest*
- ■ *yellow - yellower - the yellowest*
- ■ *friendly - friendlier - the friendliest*

More and **the most** are used to form comparatives and superlatives of adjectives of two, three or more syllables.
- ■ *modern - more modern - the most modern*

Less and **the least** are used to form comparatives and superlatives of inferiority.
- ■ *economical - less economical - the least economical*

Use the **comparative** to compare two items (it is often followed by than).
- ■ *Our new house is more convenient than the old one because it's near the shops.*

The **superlative** is used to compare one item or member of a group (of things or people) with the whole group (including that item or member).
- ■ *Ian used to be the shortest boy in his class.*

Note these irregular adjectives: **good, bad, ill, little, much, many.**

Form either comparatives or superlatives to complete the sentences. Don't forget to add <u>than</u> and <u>the</u> where necessary. Use these adjectives: *big, interesting, good, sweet, expensive, bad, ill, narrow, friendly, beautiful.*

1 I'll buy this dress because it is _____ _____ the blue one.

2 I think _____ subject to study is nuclear physics. I hate it.

3 This wine is _____ I have ever tasted.

4 He's _____ friend I've ever had.

5 We need a _____ house now that the children are older.

6 The river is quite wide here but it gets _____ further down.

7 I'm very disappointed with you. This is _____ school report you've ever had.

8 Every time I look at the scenery, it seems _____ ever.

9 It started off as a slight cold, but I feel _____ this week, doctor.

10 William is much _____ his brother. He has asked me to go sailing at the weekend.

Passive voice (Part A)

Formation: to form the passive voice use the verb **to be** in the appropriate tense and the **past participle** of the main verb. ■ *The room is being cleaned at the moment.*

i. Use **by** to introduce the agent (e.g. the person or thing responsible for the action).
- ■ *The report was written by a person I trust.*

Note: Mention the agent only if it's important to the meaning of the sentence.

ii. With the exception of the Present Continuous and Past Continuous all other continuous tenses rarely occur in the passive.

Use the passive voice:

i. when the activity done is more important than the doer (agent),
- ■ *My room has recently been redecorated.*

ii. when the doer is unknown or obvious,
- ■ *Many people were killed when the bomb exploded.*

iii. in formal language because it is associated with an impersonal style.
- ■ *The invoice will be delivered some time next week.*

┌───┐
│   **LEARNING TIPS**   │
│ Remember: If the subject does the action, use an *active verb*. │
│ If the subject receives the action, use a *passive verb*. │
└───┘

Rewrite the following sentences in the passive. Include the agent only where necessary.

1 They built this mansion in 1962.

_____

2 A Russian architect built this mansion in 1962.

_____

3 Cleaners are cleaning the offices at the moment.

_____

4 Someone has stolen my wallet.

_____

5 Scientists carry out this experiment at room temperature.

_____

6 She will type the report first thing tomorrow morning.

_____

Unit 11

Exercise 1

For questions 1 - 10, read the text below and look carefully at each line. Some of the lines are correct, and some have a word which should not be there. If a line is correct, put a tick (✓) by the number. If a line has a word that should not be there, write the word next to the number.

STRUCK BY LIGHTNING

1   According to an official statistics from England and Wales, dating from

2   1800, nearly 1,800 people have been killed before by direct lightning strikes. The

3   average number of people killed each year has, however, fallen

4   dramatically from twenty in the late 1800s, to an average of five after since

5   1960. The same pattern is repeated ever in the US. Deaths are down from

6   around three hundred a year in the 1890s to an average of ninety-five per

7   year now. This decline in casualties can to be explained by a change in

8   people's occupations. Nowadays, far more fewer people work outdoors on

9   farms, and city dwellers are protected by tall buildings and other structures

10   which attract the lightning first. People who they play sports outdoors such

     as golfers and water sports enthusiasts are now most at risk.

Exercise 2

For questions 11 - 19, read the text below. Use the word given in capitals at the end of each line to form a word that fits in the space in the same line.

GENETIC ENCODING

Every living (11) .... carries a plan in each of the cells in its body. The   ORGAN

plan is carried on pairs of chromosomes (23 in human (12) ....), which   BE

are spirally curved ribbons called DNA. Along each chromosome there are individual

pieces of (13) .... or codes called genes. It is the genes, in various   INFORM

(14) .... , that determine an animal's size and shape, the colour of its fur   COMBINE

or feathers, how good its sense of smell or (15) .... is, and how fast it   SEE

runs, flies or swims. Every animal gets half its genes from one parent and half from the

other. As each new (16) .... is produced, these bits of code are shuffled   GENERATE

like a pack of cards to give (17) .... different combinations and variations.   END

That is why brothers and sisters may often share a family (18) ....   LIKE

but are never (19) .... like either of their parents.   EXACT

Exercise 3

For questions 20 - 27, read the text below and think of the word which fits each space. Use only one word in each space.

Movie cameras have come a long way since the early days of cinema. The cameras of the beginning of the century were, for the most part, roughly made wooden boxes, which had to (20) .... wound by hand. The big change in cameras came in the 1920s along with the 'talkies' - sound films. The wooden boxes (21) .... replaced (22) .... well-built metal machines. They were also equipped (23) .... soundproof covers designed to muffle the noise of the mechanism which wound the film while the movie was (24) .... shot. Today, the basic construction of the movie camera (25) .... changed very little but some improvements have been (26) .... Now, over 300 metres of film can be stored in a 'magazine' on the top of the camera and driven through the machine by an electric motor. Some cameras are equipped with a monitoring viewfinder with a screen on which the image being photographed (27) .... reproduced. This is a useful guide for the camera operator in shots where the camera moves.

Exercise 4

For questions 28 - 32, complete the second sentence so that it has a similar meaning to the first sentence, using the word given. Do not change the word given.

28 That was the worst film I've ever seen. I've never .... than that.	worse
29 They found the sewing class the least interesting of all the courses offered. The sewing class was .... the other courses on offer.	less
30 Cyclists are not allowed to ride on the school lawns. Bicycles .... on the school lawns.	must
31 They've built these houses with a new kind of fireproof wood. These houses .... of fireproof wood.	been
32 'My Mum wouldn't let me take horseback riding lessons when I was young,' Karen said. Karen said ....horseback riding lessons when she was young.	allow

Unit 12

under - over, below - above, beneath, underneath

under means *in a position lower than; directly below; covered by*

■ *The pencil is under the book on the desk.*
■ *He lay down under the tree to rest for a while.*

over means *in a position higher than; directly above*

■ *There was a beautiful antique lamp hanging over the dining-room table.*

below means *in a lower place or on a lower level than, but not necessarily under*

■ *The Dead Sea is 397 metres below sea level.*
■ *He stood on the hill admiring the river in the valley below.*

above means *in a higher place or on a higher level than, but not necessarily over*

■ *There was a helicopter hovering above the village.*

underneath is used instead of **under** for emphasis

■ *Have you looked underneath the bed for your slippers?*

beneath means *directly under, used esp. in formal writing or in literature*

■ *The only sound that could be heard was the crunching of snow beneath my feet.*

by, with

by is used to introduce the particular method through which sth is done

■ *The vase was expensive because it was painted by hand.*
■ *He succeeded in passing his exam by working very hard.*

with is used to introduce the tools or instruments to do sth

■ *She was teaching her son how to eat with a knife and fork.*

Use <u>under</u>, <u>over</u>, <u>below</u>, <u>above</u>, <u>underneath</u>, <u>beneath</u>, <u>by</u> or <u>with</u> to fill in the gaps.

1 The valley was _____ the little village.

2 I can fix it _____ super-glue.

3 Why don't you look for your books _____ your desk?

4 This machine is operated _____ pulling the handle towards you.

5 The ship lay for many years _____ the waves.

6 Look _____ the car to check the exhaust pipe.

7 The seagull was soaring high _____ the clouds.

8 The doctor leaned _____ the little boy to check his heartbeat.

9 We could hear a quarrel going on in the flat _____ .

10 I usually clean the cracks _____ an old toothbrush.

11 This is a safety cap. You open it _____ pushing down first and then turning it.

12 There's a pile of magazines on the table. Have you looked _____ them?

13 The plane was flying _____ the clouds, so we could not see the high peaks of the Alps _____ .

---

as...as, as / so...as

as...as is used to compare people, things or ideas that are similar in some way.

■ *She is as hospitable as her mother.*

so...as is used instead of **as...as** to make negative comparisons, although this distinction tends to disappear and **as...as** can be used in all types of sentences.

■ *This cheese pie isn't as / so good as it was the last time I made it.*

Use <u>(not) as...as</u> and <u>so...as</u> to rewrite the sentences.

1 Brian is clever and so is his brother.

_____

2 My boss is richer than I am.

_____

3 Both Peter and Bob can type 45 words per minute.

_____

4 I study harder than my roommate.

_____

Passive voice (Part B)

If the active verb has two objects, a **direct object** and an **indirect object**, either of them can become the subject of the passive voice sentence, depending on where the emphasis is.

However, it is more common for the indirect object to become the subject of the passive sentence.

A direct object answers the question 'What?'; an indirect object answers the question 'To whom?' or 'For whom?'.

- *Someone bought her an expensive ring.*
- *She was bought an expensive ring.*

- *Someone taught a lesson to the whole class.*
- *A lesson was taught to the whole class.*

Rewrite the following sentences in the passive voice.

1 Someone has given me a promotion.

_____

2 A man promised Sue a job.

_____

3 Fortunately, John gave me another chance.

_____

4 People have told me several lies about you.

_____

5 Someone sent me a camera from Japan.

_____

Verbs with two objects

There are two possible structures after the verbs *give, lend, offer, pass, promise, read, sell, send, show, teach, tell:*
i. (give) somebody something
  - *Give John the book.*
ii. (give) something to somebody
  - *Give the book to John.*
Structure ii is preferred when:
a. 'somebody' consists of several words
  - *Give it to the good-looking young man.*
 b. 'something' is a pronoun (e.g. it, them)
  - *Give it to John.*

There are also two possible structures after the verbs *get, book, buy, choose, cook, cut, find, keep, make, paint, pour, prepare, save, win:*
i. (get) somebody something
  - *Get me a pen.*
ii. (get) something for somebody
  - *Get a pen for me.*
Structure ii is preferred when we want to emphasize 'somebody'.

Put the words in brackets in the right order to complete the sentences. Use both structures where possible.

1 It's raining. Can you lend (your umbrella / me)
_____?

2 He said he sold (a young couple / it)
_____.

3 Why don't you lend (the book / Mary)
_____?

4 They've managed to book (a table / his family)
_____.

5 She bought (a nice present / her mother)
_____
for her birthday.

6 Martin's mother has promised (a computer / him)
_____
if he passes the exams.

7 She always tells (a story / the children) _____
before they go to sleep at night.

8 Of course I'll make _____
_____ (a cake / you).

Exercise 1

For questions 1 - 9, read the text below and look carefully at each line. Some of the lines are correct, and some have a word which should not be there. If a line is correct, put a tick (✓) by the number. If a line has a word that should not be there, write the word next to the number.

THE GREAT CHILEAN EARTHQUAKE

1 On date May 22, 1960, a piece of rock broke somewhere beneath the coast
2 of central Chile. The crack continued to grow up wider and longer. About
3 five minutes later it stopped, it having travelled about 960 kilometres. It was
4 the most largest earthquake in the past two centuries. As the crack
5 spread, the rock on both sides moved by a total of round 20 metres and
6 the western edge of South America moved westwards. Enormous vibrations
7 were set off that shook buildings not until they were completely demolished
8 down. The movement of the sea floor also created a giant wave, known as
9 a tsunami. This great wave spread out into the Pacific, moving almost as
   fast as a jet plane. In the middle of the night, a wall of water 15 metres high
   burst over the town of Hilo on Hawaii 8,000 kilometres away.

Exercise 2

For questions 10 - 17, read the text below. Use the word given in capitals at the end of each line to form a word that fits in the space in the same line.

THE FORTUNES OF A HOUSE

Many historical homes are being 'recycled' from a faded past to a glittering present. A typical
example is a (10) .... Victorian house in London that passed through several   **BEAUTY**
stages of decay before returning to its former glory. It was (11) .... built for a rich   **ORIGINAL**
upper-class family around 1860. Fifty years later the house had changed very little except
that (12) .... had replaced gas as a means of lighting. However, by 1950 the house   **ELECTRIC**
was in very bad condition. The rooms were being rented out and (13) .... and   **DECORATE**
repairs had been largely ignored. By the mid 1970s the building was falling apart. Most of the
windows had been smashed and the rooms wrecked by vandals. The house was bought by
the local council, which hoped to redevelop the whole area, but (14) .... the   **FORTUNATE**
money ran out. The building was finally sold in the 1990s to developers specialising in 'peri-
od restoration'. Whole streets of (15) .... houses are now being converted   **ROT**
into 'luxury apartments' and sold to (16) .... buyers, changing the status of many   **WEALTH**
areas and saving examples of beautiful (17) .... for future generations.   **ARCHITECT**

Exercise 3

For questions 8 - 14, read the text below and think of the word which fits each space. Use only one word in each space.

DESTRUCTION OF FORESTS

In a Malaysian rain forest a logger switches off his chainsaw and a great tree crashes to the ground just twenty minutes after the logger started work. In that time, worldwide, an area of rain forest (18) .... big as 620 football pitches has been cut down (19) .... industrial use.
Unlike a lot of environmental damage, this cannot be reversed. Once a forest has gone, it has gone. Of course, trees can be replanted but animal and plant life in the forests cannot be recreated. However, saving the rain forests may not be as difficult (20) .... it seems. With a bit of vision and commitment politicians could put together a rescue package. Instead of cutting down trees for money, foresters can be encouraged to harvest only valuable materials; secondly, new trees can be planted. In (21) .... way, forests can be protected and the local people can earn (22) .... than they would from just cutting down trees to raise cattle. But how can we help? First, we should avoid eating hamburgers made (23) .... beef imported from rain forest countries. Second, we need to make sure we don't buy furniture made from rain forest timber unless we are sure the forests (24) .... properly managed.

Exercise 4

For questions 25 - 29, complete the second sentence so that it has a similar meaning to the first sentence, using the word given. Do not change the word given.

25 I'm sure Mr Wilson was sent the booklet.   **posted**
   I'm sure the booklet .... Mr Wilson.

26 During the accident, the tanker was damaged more seriously than the smaller ship.   **as**
   During the accident, ... the tanker.

27 Ugh! This milk's sour. How long have you had it?   **gone**
   Ugh! This milk .... How long have you had it?

28 She removed the bandage with a pair of scissors.   **by**
   She removed the bandage .... a pair of scissors .

29 When those old houses were demolished, builders found the ruins of an ancient temple below the foundations.   **torn**
   When the old houses .... , builders found the ruins of an ancient temple below the foundations.

Unit 13

Phrasal verbs

- **come about**
  happen
- **come across**
  i. find or meet by chance
  ii. give the impression of having a particular characteristic
- **come apart**
  break or collapse
- **come by**
  obtain sth unexpectedly
- **come down**
  go or fall to a lower level
- **come forward**
  present oneself
- **come off**
  succeed in happening
- **come round**
  i. visit
  ii. regain consciousness
- **come through**
  survive and recover from a dangerous situation
- **come up**
  arise as a subject
- **come up against**
  be faced with a problem
- **come up with**
  suggest an idea or plan

Fill in the gaps with the appropriate phrasal verb.

1. He _____ the operation all right.
2. I'll _____ to see you tomorrow.
3. When his name _____ during the discussion, everyone fell silent.
4. He _____ as a rude and selfish boy.
5. Two witnesses _____ to testify against the defendant.
6. The discovery of penicillin actually _____ by accident.
7. I dropped the book on the floor and its pages _____.
8. I _____ some very interesting manuscripts in the library.
9. Despite her nervousness, her performance _____ very well.
10. He _____ the most extraordinary excuse for his absence.
11. If our expenses don't _____, we'll soon face bankruptcy.
12. They _____ a problem they couldn't solve.
13. I wonder how he _____ all that money.
14. She _____ one hour after she had fainted.

What is ...like? / How...? / What does...look like?

What is ... like? is used to ask for a description of the qualities of something / someone.
- *What's your new job like?*

The answer can be a description or a comparison.
- *It's quite interesting but rather tiring.*
- *It's much more interesting than the previous one.*

How...? is used when we want:
i. to know the manner in which something is / was / will be done
- *How did you do it?*
ii. before adjectives/adverbs
- *How tall is he?*
- *How fast was he going?*

What does ... look like? is used to ask for a description of the appearance, not the character.
- *'What does he look like?'*
  'He's tall and handsome.'

Write appropriate questions for these statements.

1. _____?
   Go straight ahead to the junction and then follow the signs to Cambridge. You won't miss it.

2. _____?
   She has blond hair and a fair complexion.

3. _____?
   It was one of the best films I've ever seen.

4. _____?
   I know him very well because we've been friends since we left school.

Unit 13

the same...as , as much as, as many as

The same...as is used with **nouns** referring to:
age, colour, height, length, etc
- *My mother is the same age as my father.*

but *not* with **adjectives** such as: *old, red, tall*
- **Wrong:** *My mother is the same old as my father.*

As much as and **as many as** are often used with multiple numbers:

half, twice, three times, four times, etc
- *John ate twice as much as Andrew but drank half as many pints of beer.*

Multiple numbers always come before, not after the phrase **as much / many as.**
- *This is twice as much as I wanted.*

Use the <u>same...as</u>, <u>as much as</u> or <u>as many as</u> to rewrite the sentences.

1. Your blouse is red and mine is too. (*colour*)

_____

2. I've got $6 and he's got $3. (*money*)

_____

3. Luke's job pays him a lot of money and so does Helen's. (*salary*)

_____

4. I know a lot of people but you know more.

_____

Passive voice (Part C)

If the active sentence consists of:

subject	verb	that - clause
People	*say*	*that he is rich.*

it has two possible forms in the passive:
- *It is said that he is rich.*
  He is said to be rich.

Note the different types of infinitive used, depending on the time of the action in relation to the time of the main verb:
People expect him to come tomorrow.
- *He is expected to come tomorrow.*
People say that he died in Asia.
- *He is said to have died in Asia.*
People say that he is working hard.
- *He is said to be working hard.*
We believe that he has been working very hard recently.
- *He is believed to have been working very hard recently.*

Finish each of the sentences in such a way that it means the same as the sentence printed before it.

1. People say that he once appeared on TV.

He is _____

_____

2. Years ago, people believed that the earth was flat.

Years ago, the earth _____

_____

3. It is thought that Christopher Columbus was one of the world's greatest explorers.

Christopher Columbus _____

_____

4. The report says that several people were injured during the earthquake.

It is _____

_____

53

Unit 13

Exercise 1

For questions 1 - 8, read the text below and look carefully at each line. Some of the lines are correct, and some have a word which should not be there. If a line is correct, put a tick (✓) by the number. If a line has a word that should not be there, write the word next to the number.

CHILD CRIMINALS

1 In a case that shocked to the whole of Europe, two girls, S.Thomas and
2 J. Richards, both 13 years old, were found guilty of kidnapping and
3 murdering this four-year-old L.Davies. The two girls are the youngest
4 European subjects to be convicted of murder in during the last 250 years.
5 Thomas and Richards were sentenced to imprisonment and it is believed
6 that they will to serve a jail term of at least 25 years. The overwhelming and
7 indisputable evidence that were led to this jail sentence was a video tape of
8 the both two girls leading the four-year-old out of a sports centre and
   their subsequent confession.

Exercise 2

For questions 9 - 15, read the text below. Use the word given in capitals at the end of each line to form a word that fits in the space in the same line.

SOMETHING NEEDS TO BE DONE

Every year 20,000 species of wildlife become extinct because their habitat is being destroyed by man. It
is clear that something must be done to stop the loss of biodiversity (the (9) .... variety of   REPLACE
animal and plant life around the globe). In order to do this, countries must identify (10) ....   DANGER
species and protect the places where they live. A lot of countries need (11) .... help so   FINANCE
when a company manufactures a medicine using the ingredients from a rare plant or animal, it should
share the profits with the country where the (12) .... was made. Nothing is being done to   DISCOVER
stop logging companies, (13) .... and land speculators from chopping down or burning   SETTLE
(14) .... forests where a lot of these rare species live. Something needs to be done before   TROPIC
all the (15) .... treasures of these forests are destroyed.   BIOLOGY

Exercise 3

For questions 16 - 23, read the text below and think of the word which fits each space. Use only one word in each space.

CHILDREN AND THE LAW

In Britain, a child below the age of 10 cannot (16) .... found guilty of a criminal offence, which means the breaking of a rule or law. Children (17) .... the ages of 10-14 (18) .... be convicted of crimes if it can be (19) .... that they knew what they were doing was wrong. Children from 14 and over (20) .... assumed to know as much about crime and the law (21) .... an adult.

In other words, when they are arrested for a crime, their case is decided in a Juvenile Court (22) .... law, (a special court that tries young people). (23) .... 17 a child becomes an adult in the eyes of the law.

Exercise 4

For questions 24 - 28, complete the second sentence so that it has a similar meaning to the first sentence, using the word given. Do not change the word given.

24 This tin contains 500 grams of coffee but that tin contains less coffee.   **much**
   That tin .... this tin.

25 'What does that new synthetic fur feel like?' she asked.   **felt**
   She wanted .... like.

26 They say that the questions that have been included in this week's test are the same as last week's.   **said**
   It .... in this week's test are the same as last week's test.

27 They believe that the ship, which was supposedly carrying supplies, actually
   had a cargo consisting of drugs and lethal weapons.   **is**
   It .... which was supposedly carrying supplies,
   actually had a cargo consisting of drugs and lethal weapons.

28 'How did the suspect who was carrying the gun come to your attention?' he asked the witness.   **noticed**
   The witness .... the suspect who had been carrying the gun.

Unit 14

Phrasal verbs

turn back
    stop and return to the place one
    began a journey from

turn...down
    i. reject sb or sth
    ii. (of a hi-fi, heater) reduce the
        volume or the intensity

turn...into
    make sth different

turn into
    become different

turn...off
    (of a machine, engine, appliance, etc)
    cause to stop working

turn...on
    (of a machine, engine, appliance, etc)
    cause to start working

turn out
    be the result in the end

turn to
    ask for help or advice

turn up
    arrive

Fill in the gaps with the appropriate phrasal verb.

1 Although the party got off to an uncomfortable start, it _____ fine in the end.

2 She was furious to see her ex-boyfriend _____ unexpectedly at her party.

3 I think we're lost. We'll have to _____.

4 The ugly frog suddenly _____ a handsome prince.

5 Have you got anyone to _____ when you are in need of advice?

6 She politely _____ his proposal of marriage.

7 Don't forget to _____ your computer before you leave.

8 It's hot in here. _____ the temperature _____, please.

9 I can't _____ the lights; we must have blown a fuse.

10 Water _____ ice at zero degrees Celsius.

like, as

Like and **as** may be used in comparisons.
As is followed by:
i. a clause to compare one action with another,
   ■ *He typed it exactly as I had instructed.*
ii. a noun to say what sb is or was (esp. when talking about jobs) and how sth is used or done.
   ■ *It's my responsibility, as your teacher, to tell you what to do.*

Like + noun / pronoun / gerund means *the same as or similar to.*
   ■ *The little girl was trembling like a leaf when she got up to recite her poem.*
   ■ *When he realised he was being followed, he started running like a deer.*

Compare:
   ■ *As a teacher, I advise you to work harder.*
     (=In my capacity as a teacher. I am a teacher.)
   ■ *Like your teacher, I advise you to work harder.*
     (=I am not a teacher, but I advise you, as your teacher does, to work harder.)

In some of the sentences below there are mistakes. Correct the mistakes.

1 He tried to solve the problem like his teacher had shown him.

_____

2 Don't touch anything. Leave everything like it is until the police arrive.

_____

3 Like mother, like daughter. (English proverb)

_____

4 Stop behaving as a child.

_____

5 He used to work as a builder but he has now found a better paid job.

_____

much, very

Much is used with comparative adjectives or adverbs.
My new car is much better than my old one.

Very is used with adjectives or adverbs in the affirmative.
'My niece is a very clever girl,' he said proudly.

Use either <u>much</u> or <u>very</u> to fill in the gaps.

1 She is _____ friendlier than her sister.

2 John is _____ clever.

3 They are _____ fast learners.

4 Sue is a _____ better driver than her husband.

Have / Get something done

Have / Get something done (Causative Form) is used:

i. when the subject is not the actual doer of the action but the one who arranges for sb else (usually a professional or specialist) to do sth for the subject,
   ■ *She had her skirt shortened.*

ii. when sth happens to sb, especially if it is unpleasant.
   ■ *He had his briefcase stolen.*

When **have** is used in the causative form, the question and negative in the Present Simple and Past Simple tenses are formed with **do/does, did.**
   ■ *How often do you have your car serviced?*

Note: Get is more informal than **have.**

Use the CAUSATIVE FORM to finish each of the following sentences in such a way that it means the same as the sentence printed before it.

1 I need a haircut.
I have to _____

2 A baker made a cake for their wedding.
They _____

3 We must ask someone to paint the house.
We must _____

4 Someone made the curtains for the Smiths' living room.
The Smiths _____

Get

get something means *have, receive, obtain, buy*
   ■ *He got a letter from his father a few days ago.*

get + adjective means: *become*
   ■ *She got very angry when she saw her daughter's report card.*

get to + place means: *arrive at a place*
   ■ *He got to the airport five minutes after the departure of his plane.*

But: What time did you get home/there/here?

get + past participle is used instead of the verb **to be** to form the passive when the verb **to be** may cause confusion.

Compare:
They were married five years ago. (=*This might mean that the wedding could have taken place before then.*)
They got married five years ago. (=*This refers to when the wedding took place.*)

Rewrite the following sentences using: <u>get</u>

1 She has asked me to buy some food for her on my way back from the office.

_____

2 Take your coat because it's colder today than yesterday.

_____

3 Someone hurt the goalkeeper during the match.

_____

4 Fortunately, the bus arrived at the station a few minutes after the explosion.

_____

5 It's easy to lose your way in the forest.

_____

Unit 14

Exercise 1

For questions 1 - 9, read the text below and look carefully at each line. Some of the lines are correct, and some have a word which should not be there. If a line is correct, put a tick (✓) by the number. If a line has a word that should not be there, write the word next to the number.

SCIENTIFIC FASHION

1 Parisians have always been ready to adopt new and exciting fashions, not
2 just in clothing but also and in thought. Throughout the centuries they have
3 got their inspiration apart from kings and queens, scientists and philosophers. In the
4 early eighteenth century, Benjamin Franklin showed that the lightning
5 was a release of electricity; this, in turn, it led to the development of
6 lightning conductors, and, for high society in Paris, not just on rooftops! In
7 the late 1770s, when interest in electricity became to widespread, the ladies
8 and gentlemen of Paris considered that it necessary to have a lightning
9 conductor attached to their hat when they went out walking. Of course,
having such a device dangling from your hat to the ground was not only
considered a safety precaution but the height of Parisian fashion.

Exercise 2

For questions 10 - 16, read the text below. Use the word given in capitals at the end of each line to form a word that fits in the space in the same line.

PASSING ON NEW IDEAS

In humans the (10) .... between various cultures is very clear. In different   **DIFFER**
parts of the world people wear different clothes, eat different food, and so on. Various
groups of people also have customs and traditions which have been handed down
through the (11) .... Animals, like humans, also have various cultural   **GENERATE**
(12) .... which are passed from one animal to another. As in humans, the   **CHARACTER**
cultural differences between one animal group and another are often very easy to see. One
famous example of the (13) .... of differing cultures in animal groups   **EXIST**
involved the passing on of a 'new (14) ....' . It was made by a member of   **PROCEED**
an (15) .... monkey colony living by the sea in Japan. One monkey found   **EXPERIMENT**
that by washing sweet potatoes she could remove sand from them and get a much better
taste. It was not long before other monkeys in the group started copying her technique.
This (16) .... is now widespread throughout the colony.   **BEHAVE**

Exercise 3

For questions 17 - 24, read the text below and think of the word which fits each space. Use only one word in each space.

DISASTER DATE?

I had arranged to (17) .... Joan up at seven. I stood outside her house holding a fresh bouquet of flowers in my trembling hands. I took a deep breath and knocked. Joan opened the door and said, 'Hi. I'll just (18) .... my coat and then we can go.' In the car I felt unusually tense and for a couple of kilometres the only thing that kept the conversation going were two ridiculous remarks about the rainy weather. I was beginning to relax when suddenly the engine stopped. And there was something else: my feet and ankles felt damp and cold. We had driven into a flooded road. I turned (19) .... apologise but Joan was sitting there laughing, with her feet on the seat. We got out and started pushing. Fifteen minutes later we (20) .... the engine started. Joan turned to me smiling, 'There's no way we're going to (21) .... to the cinema on time. And we really must get some dry clothes on. Why don't you (22) .... me home?' What a disaster! I hadn't even managed a simple thing (23) .... taking my date to the movies. When we (24) .... to her house, we were both shivering with cold. She asked me in and we spent the rest of the evening talking in front of the fire. Three weeks later she agreed to marry me.

Exercise 4

For questions 25 - 29, complete the second sentence so that it has a similar meaning to the first sentence, using the word given. Do not change the word given.

25	Long journeys often tire me.	**get**
	I often .... long journeys.	
26	Everyone at the party was surprised when the Prince arrived unexpectedly.	**turned**
	Everyone at the party was surprised when	
27	The flight attendant asked him if he had had his passport checked at the air terminal.	**have**
	'.. at the air terminal?' asked the flight attendant.	
28	Oh, dear! I forgot that it was my turn to collect the kids from school!	**pick**
	Oh dear! I forgot that it was my turn to .... from school!	
29	Will you be able to get to your house on your own?	**home**
	Will you be able to .... on your own?	

Unit 15

Phrasal verbs

get along (with)
  have a good relationship with
get ... across
  cause sth to be communicated
  or understood
get away
  escape
get away (with)
  avoid punishment
get ... back
  regain possession of
get by
  survive; manage
get ... down
  depress
get on with
  i. start or continue doing sth
  ii. have a good relationship with
get out of
  escape or avoid doing sth
get over
  recover from an illness or other
  unpleasant experience
get round to
  find the time to do sth
get through
  i.   communicate with sb by phone
  ii. pass an examination
  iii. spend or reach the end of
get to
  arrive at a place
get together
  meet

Fill in the gaps with an appropriate phrasal verb.

1. Let's _____ one evening after work.
2. Rainy weather always _____ me _____.
3. Quick! The thieves are _____.
4. We finally _____ her place at midnight.
5. How does he _____ on so little money?
6. She doesn't _____ well _____ her boss.
7. I haven't been able to _____ to him; his line is busy.
8. She managed to _____ the message _____ to her students.
9. I'll do the washing up when I _____ it.
10. I lent Mary my history book and I must _____ it _____ before the weekend.
11. I can't go swimming; I've just _____ a bad cold.
12. My sister always manages to _____ doing the ironing.
13. Please, _____ your work, children.
14. You'll never _____ this!
15. We'll have _____ replying to all these letters by the end of the day.
16. Do you _____ well _____ your teacher?
17. Don't worry. You'll easily _____ your driving test.

as if / as though

As if / As though are used
interchangeably to describe how
someone or something looks, sounds,
tastes or behaves.

■ *He acted as if / as though he was mad.*
■ *You look as though / as if you are
  going to faint.*

Rewrite these sentences with as if / as though.

1. George looks very excited. I think he's won a fortune in the lottery.

   _____

2. She is so pale. She is probably ill.

   _____

3. This cheese smells awful. It's probably gone off.

   _____

too, very, enough

Too before adjectives or adverbs suggest that it is so much so that something negative comes as a result.

- *He works too slowly to have it ready in a week.*

Very is an intensifier which means to a high degree, but does not necessarily imply a negative result.

- *He works very slowly.*

Enough follows adjectives or adverbs but comes before nouns and is used:

i. with adjectives or adverbs meaning so much so that something positive comes as a result,
- *He arrived early enough to catch the train.*
- *He's clever enough to understand.*

ii. with nouns meaning so much of it or so many of them / us / you that something positive comes as a result.
- *There's enough food for everyone.*

Use too, very, or enough to fill in the gaps.

1. I have _____ money to go abroad.

2. He is _____ lazy to pass the exam.

3. I'm not tall _____ to reach the ceiling.

4. Although he tried _____ hard, he didn't pass the driving test.

5. Working in such an environment can be _____ dangerous.

6. It's _____ early to tell, but there shouldn't be any problems.

7. It's an X-rated film so we're not old _____ to see it.

8. The plane leaves _____ early in the morning. Should we ask for a later flight?

Future Perfect vs. Future Perfect Continuous

The **Future Perfect (I will have done)** is used:
i. for an action that will happen before a particular time in the future or before another future action. The result of the action will come up to the point of future time which is mentioned, or up to the time of the second action
- *I will have finished by the time you come.*

ii. with **just** to describe an action that will have been completed only a short time before the point of future time mentioned, or before the time of the second action
- *We will have just started eating at that time.*

iii. with **for** to describe a situation that began in the past, or will begin in the future, and will still be in effect at a later time in the future
- *They will have been married for two years this coming June.*

The **Future Perfect Continuous (I will have been doing)** is used:
for an action which will be in progress at a certain moment of future time, but which goes backwards in time for a period of time introduced by **for**.
- *She will have been studying English for three years by the end of this term.*

Note: By, in the context of the example above, means: *no later than* and is a preposition. The phrase **by the time** is used as a conjunction to introduce time clauses.

Correct the mistakes, where necessary.

1. By next month, my father will be working for thirty years as a primary school teacher.

_____

2. In May 2008, I will have been knowing my husband for fifteen years.

_____

3. Tom will have just arrived home when the football match begins.

_____

4. I will have finished the housework by two o'clock, so I'll be able to study.

_____

5. When will you have been finishing? I'm in a hurry.

_____

6. I will have written this book for three years by this time next week.

_____

Exercise 1

For questions 1 - 11, read the text below and look carefully at each line. Some of the lines are correct, and some have a word which should not be there. If a line is correct, put a tick (✓) by the number. If a line has a word that should not be there, write the word next to the number.

WEDDING ORGANISERS

1	Are you thinking of the big day? Will you have been arranged everything for
2	the ceremony and reception as well as and still kept your sanity? If things
3	seem too overwhelming for you and you're not getting enough sleep, if all
4	the stresses of the preparations are making you feel like as though your life
5	is getting enough out of control, then you might want to contact us at
6	Wedding Organisers. We will have take care of everything for your wedding
7	and reception from helping you too choose your wedding dress to booking the
8	church, from sending wedding invitations to the decorating the cake so that
9	you and your husband-to-be will look like the perfect couple you are.
10	There's no need for you to look and feel exhausted and not enjoy the most
11	very important day of your life. All you have to do is find Mr Right and we'll
	take care of the rest.

Exercise 2

For questions 12 - 18, read the text below. Use the word given in capitals at the end of each line to form a word that fits in the space in the same line.

FUTURE PERFECT?

What will shopping be like in the year 2050? Will supermarkets have (12) ....   APPEAR

by that time? Or will they have become even more complex? Some (13) ....   SEARCH

believe that many changes will have taken place by the year 2050 and that shopping on the

whole will have become a more convenient and (14) .... pursuit. One change   PLEASURE

that will have taken place by then is the (15) .... of satellite radio in grocers'   INTRODUCE

where in-store radio networks will broadcast ads and store specials with music in between.

Another convenience will be the (16) .... of faxes in nearly all chain stores so   INSTALL

that customers can send their grocery lists and have goods delivered straight to their homes.

And of course, we will have the extra (17) .... of cashless shopping, in that all   CONVENIENT

shops will accept credit cards or debit cards so that we won't have to carry cash around with

us. It seems as though technology will even have got rid of the (18) .... type   BAD

of shoppers - pick pockets.

Exercise 3

For questions 19 - 28, read the text below and think of the word which fits each space. Use only one word in each space.

THE ERRORS OF OUR DEEDS

The rate (19) .... extinction of dinosaurs was very slow compared (20) .... what is happening on our planet today. Current rates (21) .... extinction and the number of endangered animals disappearing is (22) .... higher than at any other time in the Earth's long history. Dinosaurs vanished (23) .... the face of the earth through natural events, however, today, thousands of species are becoming extinct mainly (24) .... of the increase of just one species - man. (25) .... the last 400 years, approximately 35 species of mammal and 95 species of bird have (26) .... extinct.

According to scientists, at least another 120 more mammals and nearly 1,000 birds (27) .... have disappeared by the year 2020 if man continues to dominate their world through greed, lack of thought and disregard for situations that we think are (28) .... our control.

Exercise 4

For questions 29 - 33, complete the second sentence so that it has a similar meaning to the first sentence, using the word given. Do not change the word given.

29 It will take her four weeks to finish her English composition.   **working**

She .... English composition for four weeks by the time she finishes it.

30 This flat isn't big enough for all of us.   **too**

This flat .... for all of us.

31 He looks as though he's lost his best friend.   **if**

He .... he's lost his best friend.

32 That detective's speciality is to find people who have gone missing.   **good**

That detective .... people who have gone missing.

33 The dodo is one of many species of bird that has died out.   **extinct**

The dodo is one of many species of bird ....